UNLOCKING MOMENTUM

**THE CIO'S KEYS TO
ACCELERATING CHANGE AND
BECOMING A STRATEGIC C-LEVEL PARTNER**

UNLOCKING MOMENTUM

THE CIO'S KEYS TO ACCELERATING CHANGE AND BECOMING A STRATEGIC C-LEVEL PARTNER

AARON KOPEL

Niche Pressworks
Indianapolis, IN

UNLOCKING MOMENTUM: THE CIO'S KEYS TO ACCELERATING
CHANGE AND BECOMING A STRATEGIC C-LEVEL PARTNER
Copyright © 2025 by Aaron Kopel

For permission to reprint portions of this content or for bulk purchases,
contact books@projectbrilliant.com

Published by Niche Pressworks; NichePressworks.com
Indianapolis, IN

ISBN
Paperback: 978-1-962956-42-0
Hardback: 978-1-962956-39-0
eBook: 978-1-962956-43-7

Library of Congress Cataloging-in-Publication Data on File at lccn.loc.gov

This book is dedicated to the many clients over the years who have allowed me to take part in their incredible journey as they transform their mindsets and their businesses to meet the demands of a rapidly changing environment.

The experiences we've shared have been some of the best parts of my career, and I've thoroughly enjoyed watching you meet every new challenge like the championship teams I knew you could be. I look forward to remaining the most enthusiastic guy in your cheering section for many years to come.

CONTENTS

INTRODUCTION

THE CIO'S DILEMMA

Being a CIO in today's rapidly shifting economy isn't for the weak at heart. Navigating lightning-fast changes in technology, executing huge, complex projects with multiple moving parts, and helping internal partners meet business goals while managing risk and budgets make the role a complex and sometimes daunting adventure.

To cope, many CIOs adopt tried-and true-practices that have for years been lauded as the gold standard in business, and yet these traditional methods don't seem to measure up in meeting today's challenges.

Meanwhile, IT remains one of business's best positioned and most equipped areas to enable gains in innovation and business agility. A CIO who is able to lead change effectively is also uniquely situated to become a change leader throughout the organization, creating a culture of collaboration and innovation. The potential business outcomes speak for themselves — greater customer value and satisfaction, better market adaptation, and product-centric strategy that allows expansion into previously unknown or unexplored markets, to name a few.

With this potential in mind, it's time for the CIO to take a new role, expanding his or her leadership to become a solid, vital partner in the C-suite. That requires, first and foremost, a new mindset: ready not only to cope with change but to anticipate and welcome it. Any leader with this mindset will be well equipped not only to take his or her organization to the next level of excellence but to help redefine excellence in new and exciting ways.

Through these pages, you'll learn how to:

- redefine the business problems you're dealing with,
- set a new vision for greater business agility,
- work within a viable framework for change,
- start down the transformation path yourself (beginning with your own mindset as a leader for change), and
- become an indispensable partner for growth, change, and innovation with senior leadership and your peers.

Somewhere along the road, you'll realize that instead of seeking the comforting and predictable world of traditional business practices and metrics, you'd rather be the first to head down the next new road, embracing the unknown, not as the next potential threat, but as the next important discovery. And if you've embodied the right leadership mindset and practices, there's a good chance your peers and team will be ready and able to set off with you.

If this sounds intriguing, read on. There's a lot to do, and you're the one who can do it.

LOCKED IN A DYSFUNCTIONAL LOOP

CHAPTER 1

A NEW PERSPECTIVE ON AN OLD PROBLEM

Erroneous assumptions can be disastrous.
— PETER DRUCKER

Perry wasn't my usual kind of client.

First off, I'd known him since 2012. We'd worked together at a long-term care insurance company, where he had brought me in as a consultant before I moved on to a different client in the financial sector on the east coast.

That pre-knowledge was part of why he was different. But the most important thing that was different from most of my clients was that he actually knew he needed my help, and he already knew why.

He and I often met for coffee (me)/tea (him) for years now, and it was back in 2018, during one of these catching-up meetings, when he told me his dilemma.

He'd recently been hired on as the CIO for the company where he'd previously been in a trial position as a 1099 contractor, and he was excited about his new position. As we settled into our seats in the coffee shop, he told me about one of his first major projects: swapping out their core insurance policy management system — a twenty-year-old legacy system — for a better modern one.

It was a giant project with a bunch of tentacles, and he was still trying to wrap his head around it.

"What's your timeframe?" I asked, temporarily popping the lid off my cup so the piping-hot coffee could cool off enough to drink.

"You know how it goes," he said. "You do a three-year project plan, and it turns into a five-year project plan." Perry rolled his eyes, then took a sip of his Earl Grey. "I don't want to wait till Year Three to make key decisions and then find out we have two more years to go."

"So you're shooting for three years?"

"Well, I hope not," he said, grinning. "That's why I'm talking to you. But who knows? There are a lot of moving parts. There's a company we outsource customer service to in India whose contract is up for renewal in a few months, and I'm trying to decide whether or not to keep them through this shift. It's going to add a lot more complexity if we do, but maybe it will be easier to keep them versus hiring someone who isn't already familiar with us.

"Plus, we're already worried about the data migration. I'm pretty sure we'll have some major data cleaning to do, just based on what we're already seeing." He went on to describe several other variables that might factor in in unknown ways.

Finally, he said, "The basic problem is that there's a huge pile of stuff to do, and it's all getting in its own way. And I don't think we can tackle it using the usual ways of doing things."

As he talked, I nodded. I'd been here before, many times.

"So what you're telling me is that this isn't just about moving into this new system," I said. "What you really need is to transform the way your entire area is doing business to become much more effective," I said.

He nodded. "That's it."

I pondered this for a few moments, thinking about all the moving parts. He'd need some partnerships to accomplish what he wanted, so that was the next thing to assess. "I assume you're good with your boss since she just hired you, but what about peers?" I asked. "Can you pull in allies easily?"

"Well, sure; the CEO is supporting me. But she's new in her job, too. So she's still getting her feet wet — she doesn't really know the challenges we're facing yet herself. As for my peers, a lot of the people I'd be teaming up with in other departments are newer. Some of those positions are even vacant. So, who knows who'll be coming in? But we need to get going on it anyway — I can't wait for them to be hired. And that's another reason why I want your help. We need to start this thing off right and keep it moving well."

I was definitely interested. We talked more, and I told him I'd put together a rough pitch and a quote for the preliminary project.

"I know it's not going to end there," he said, grinning. "I'm sure it's just a beginning. There's a lot more to transform, and I know it doesn't happen overnight."

"Well, we have to start somewhere," I said. Then I returned his smile, appreciating the fact that he was definitely an easier sell since we had already been through this together in the past. "But at least you know you're in for a longer haul. I usually have more educating to do with new clients." I paused.

Then, I brought up the most important point. "There is one thing we'll need you to start thinking about right away. Let's look for a minute beyond the challenges you're facing in your organization. Those things are going to come and go. Instead, let's look at you. How do you want to lead? What are the individual internal barriers holding you back from leading that way? And how do you get moving? What can you start doing on Day One to set things in motion? If you haven't thought about these things, we'll need to get them straight so you have a clear path forward through all of the challenges — even ones you haven't thought of yet."

He took this in, and I could see the wheels turning in his mind. "I've thought about that in some ways, too," he said. "I want transparency. I want to be collaborative and pull stakeholders in where they can add value and feel like they have a say in how things are working. I want to make sure we have clear communication." He thought some more. "I also want to establish trust. Some of the stakeholders are already assuming I'm just the new guy who'll be just like the last guy — nothing will move fast enough, and they won't have what they need. I'd like to change that."

I nodded. "What do you really want instead? How do you view yourself in the organization — if you had an ideal?"

He thought for a moment. "You know — it's weird, but IT always seems to be seen as a cost center. But we have so much potential to partner with our internal stakeholders to do things for them they may not even have thought of. I think most of all, I want to be a partner at the table when big decisions are made — and I want to feel like when I make promises, I can deliver.

"I want to prove all the myths are wrong about IT," he went on. "We're not the gatekeepers. We're the problem solvers and the go-to people for innovative ideas. That's where I want to be in the eyes of the C-suite and my peers."

I was grinning now. This was something I wanted to see, too. "I think we can make that happen," I told him. "If you're willing to do the work."

"You know I am," he said. A handshake and a one-arm bro hug sealed the deal as we ended our meeting.

As I headed for my office, I felt that surge of adrenaline I always get when I hear about a new engagement where I can make a real impact. The wheels had already begun turning in my head.

It wasn't just a start — it was a jump start for Perry in his new role and a great opportunity for us to really help his new organization. As I headed back to talk to my team, I knew we would hit the ground running.

Not only did Perry do the work, he and his team ended up achieving all their goals in much less time than originally predicted, and under budget. The rest of the leadership team was stunned. Many of them started asking how they could do that in their units, too.

It was definitely a success — and the main reason wasn't because Perry adopted new processes or changed up his teamwork. The main reason was that Perry started to look at the landscape with a different set of eyes than he had started out with, and that perspective gave him a huge advantage he hadn't had before.

THE "USUAL" BUSINESS PROBLEMS

If you're like Perry, you have probably defined a lot of your daily challenges already. You may see a lot of problems, but the solutions don't feel clear. You may know you need something. You're just not sure exactly what.

You've probably defined your problem as whether/how you're able to meet specific business goals or expectations. This makes sense; that's how you're being evaluated.

In your mind, your problem may fall into one or more of several different categories:

- You feel your team is too slow and can't get things done.
- You feel your team needs to be more efficient.
- Your business priorities are constantly shifting.
- You're unable to adapt to changing market demands.
- You're too hampered by regulations to be innovative or fast.
- You have a complicated situation that you need to address more quickly than you feel you can.

Whatever the defined reason, the most important fact is that if you're reading this book, your area isn't performing as desired in some way, and none of the usual solutions seem to be helping anymore. You've started getting curious and looking around for new ways to address these problems.

Maybe you feel a little like Perry — you're dealing with a lot of moving parts that aren't necessarily lining up, leaving the whole group stuck and not moving at all. Or maybe you're feeling like you're stuck in a reactive situation where you're constantly trying to meet demands that keep changing. You want to do more and be seen as more capable, and you're looking for a new way to approach the challenge.

Whatever your situation is in relation to the above, what you need is a key to unlock the momentum — you're just not sure where to find it.

If that's true, this is the book you need.

SEEING DIFFERENTLY

Looking at the issues identified above, it seems like we're identifying them logically. However, let's take a step back for a moment and take a different approach.

What if these problems are not really the true problems but rather symptoms of the underlying problem we haven't seen yet?

That underlying issue may be a clue to why none of the old solutions are working.

Part of the key to unlocking this problem is gaining the ability to differentiate between *complicated* and *complex*. People often use these terms interchangeably, but they're not the same.

The difference is that in a complicated situation, while there may be a lot of pieces and parts to the problem, we can usually find ways to fit them all together. However, in a complex situation, we are dealing with change. Those two situations are wildly different and require wildly different approaches to successfully address them.

Leaders often think they're in a *complicated* problem space, but they're actually in a *complex* one.

Here's an example. If we just throw a whole set of Legos on the floor, give you a diagram of something to build, and say, "Figure it out," that's a complicated situation. There are a lot of pieces to sort through, but if you have experience and understanding of Legos, you can make sense of it and find a solution.

But let's say we toss only half the Legos on the floor and give you a building diagram. Then, as you're working, we randomly start throwing in new and different Legos and also take some of the others away. Then, we change out the diagram of a building for a boat. Now, that's complex.

The difference between complicated and complex is *change*.

That's the world business leaders really live in every day. It's complex but is often mistaken for complicated. They think they can just use their smarts and figure it out, but that doesn't work because they don't have all the information, and the needs and goals keep changing. They're trying to apply solutions that are built for complicated problems, where the leader feels they can engineer their way out of it. But the situation is complex, and the leader doesn't have control over all the parts or what's changing.

That's why being good at managing and operating the business with KPIs and traditional problem-solution approaches is only partly effective. It doesn't work in a dynamic, shifting environment. When change is needed, an instigator and change agent is also needed. This is someone who recognizes when things need to change.

Once your mindset shifts to accept and welcome change, you realize the way you're trying to solve the problem won't work because it isn't based on the true problem. You'll need a new way.

When you realize that, everything else starts to change, too.

> Leaders often think they're in a **complicated** problem space and believe they just need to be smarter to manage all the parts, but they're actually in a **complex** situation in which they need to deal with change and adapt more effectively. **The difference between complicated and complex is *change*.**

SOME IMPORTANT QUESTIONS

Those "usual problems" on our previous list are all symptoms of bigger, underlying problems. To get to those, you have to be willing to confront some big questions.

- What if the problem isn't what you think it is? What if it's something that requires far more change than you first thought? Are you willing to commit to that? What will happen if you stop short?
- What if solving it requires you to get out of your comfort zone? Are you ready for that?

- What if it requires risk? How much risk are you comfortable with, and what level of certainty do you need to pull the trigger?
- What if it requires you to go through a period where you don't have ready answers to senior leadership's questions? Will you be able to deal with that?
- What if you need to think completely differently and change behaviors and patterns you've used for decades? Are you willing to put in that mental and emotional work?

The key to solving your problems is having the courage to answer these questions with a "yes." If you did, read on.

But if you didn't — if the answer to any of these questions is "no," then still, read on.

OK, I get it. Why read this book if you don't think it will help? It's your choice, obviously. But you might learn something that will change those no's into yeses. If you could use this information to transform your organization in ways you can't see yet, what have you got to lose but a couple of hours of reading? If you're willing to commit to that, that's a yes I can work with.

Before we start solving your real problem, though, let me tell you a little more about why I'm writing this book, so you'll see where I'm coming from.

CHAPTER 2

WHO AM I?

LIFE LESSON PART 1:
SAME PIZZA, DIFFERENT NIGHT

I needed to get up and stretch, but I tried to ignore it. I had been hunched over my keyboard for hours, looking through the project schedule. A bunch of emails were still sitting in my inbox, unread and unopened. Despite their pinging, I didn't have time to open them because I was too busy trying to figure out why the new dates weren't lining up. The software I was using should have calculated them for me, but it relied on me to enter all the stages correctly. I scanned through again. There it was — I'd overlooked a whole segment near the middle of the project and a dependency from the customer support team.

Finally! I wearily fixed my error, taking another sip of Mountain Dew to fortify myself with artificial energy. As I moused over to click on the components I needed to move, I barely registered the fact that my fingers slid around on the top of the mouse due to the grease that was still on it from last night's pizza. My keyboard was also less than hygienic. As I brushed a speck of pepperoni off it, I tried to remember the last time I ate something besides pizza for dinner.

We'd been in the office till eleven the night before, and the night before that, and the night before that... I couldn't remember how many nights back it went. Maybe forever. I had started to think I had always worked there and I had never had any sleep. It was always the same routine, day in, day out. It was a corporate version of hell, but at 22, I had the right combination of physical fortitude and mental naïveté to take it in stride. This was just what you did. Right?

My office was in a funky newer building up on the north side of Indianapolis. I was sort of lucky in that my team — ecommerce — was newer, and we were in a freshly redesigned office space on the top floor where the executives were. We were the only ones from IT in that part of the building. It was a mashup of IT and marketing.

The other workspaces in the building had the usual tan, dingy, six-foot-tall cubicles — you know the ones I mean. High enough that you don't talk to anyone for eight hours a day, and then you just go home.

But we had modern-style, open-format pods, each seating four people. It was collaborative; you could turn your head and talk to others instead of having to make an effort to get up and go out of your cubicle. We sat in cool new Herman Miller chairs, used laptops versus the desktop computers everyone else had, and had bigger monitors and better desks.

It was like a tech startup, even though we were inside an 85,000-person global manufacturing behemoth. It was everything you could want in an office where you spent most of your waking life.

Which we did.

Our average workday was 6:00 a.m. to 9:00, 10:00, even 11:00 p.m. every day, six days a week. Nobody thought twice about it. It was just what was expected. If you showed up at 7:00 a.m., everyone would ask if you were sick.

Nobody else in the building worked these hours. In spring and summer, when the days were longer, it wasn't so bad, but in fall and winter, if I was the first one in, I'd wind my way through the dark offices and hallways, turning on lights here and there. When I left, it was back through the same dark offices and hallways, turning off lights here and there if they were still on. They usually weren't. Other people had lives. They were gone long before we left.

Like I said, I was in my early twenties, so I could take the hours. I had just moved to the area, and I didn't have any other friends to go out with. I didn't have a wife or family to go home to. So I didn't really think much about it back then.

Now that I had figured out my schedule issue, I finally took a minute to stretch the kinks out of my back. That day was like any other day. We were working on a big part of the project — converting our mainframe data for use with the website. We were held up on the part we needed to work on next as we waited for another department to complete their piece of the puzzle. I was trying to reshuffle another section of the project — the product returns process — so we could keep moving, even though that wasn't really planned to be worked on yet. And it was going to be tough, because we really should finish out the component we were stuck on before doing the other. With this reverse order, we'd have to do the equivalent of bolting on stuff later. But we had to keep things moving, so we made the best of it.

Just as I'd finished my stretch and started to open my emails, our boss, Steve, came hurrying into the room. "Hey everyone, let's head to the conference room," he said. "I've got some news."

My heart sank. I knew that tone. What was it this time?

We got to use the high-end executive conference room whenever we wanted after hours. Twelve of us sank into the swanky chairs, the fresh smell of newer leather wafting up around us as we waited for whatever bad news we knew we'd be getting.

Steve started talking in that voice he used when he knew we were going to be pissed. "OK, I was down talking to Joe on the mainframe team, and he said their team won't have the configuration we need completed for at least another month. They got a new set of requirements from one of our major retailers to match the retailer's new system upgrade." He went on to describe why that was determined to be more important. It was no surprise, with him having been on that team in his previous role, that he compromised in their favor yet again so as not to rock their boat.

Kevin, one of my teammates who had more experience (and less patience) than I did, said, "Why are we just finding out about this now?"

"Well, like I said, I was just down talking to Joe, and their whole situation has changed. They have some new requests, and they need to get those done ASAP."

"Can't they just give us access to make changes ourselves?" asked Roberta, another teammate who'd been around the block a few more times than I had. "We're only three months away from launching the new site. All the other teams, like marketing, shipping, and warehousing, are coordinating to hit that date. This will set us back at least four more months and throw everything up in the air."

Steve held up his hand placatingly. "Look, I know it's a setback, but we need to give them the benefit of the doubt. They're on a tight deadline. And by the way, I also talked to Andy in marketing and let him know we're going to be a little behind. He said it's OK as long as we make up the time before launch. Oh — and they said they want to meet next week about some new things they need for customizing the user profile to auto-suggest some upsell opportunities based on their browsing patterns. So, anyways... we should be fine, right?"

I felt an odd combination of things at that point. I agreed with Steve — I knew what they were doing was important to keep the big retailer happy. But Kevin and Roberta were right, too. It seemed we were always being held to an unreasonable schedule we had absolutely no control over and kept finding out that we were delivering the wrong thing, too late, and with too much work already put in on it. We never seemed to be able to get anything done. I felt my chest tighten with frustration, realizing the schedule I'd just agonized over for two hours was now obliterated. I'd have to start over again.

And I started to wonder: wasn't there a better way?

But Steve was already fielding everyone's objections like usual, dodging past our unhappy expressions with more placating hand gestures and apologetic expressions. He wasn't the greatest manager, but he really was a nice guy, and he meant well. Even if I was the temperamental kind, which I'm not, it would be hard to hate him. Everyone in the company liked him — his team just hated how he managed things.

And then, finally, he asked us the same old question. "OK, what kind of pizza does everyone want?"

And as we put together our pizza order, that was the end of the meeting. We went back to our desks in silence (me) or muttering angrily to each other in whispers (Roberta and Kevin), waiting for the conciliatory dinner. It was our reward (aka, bribe) for staying there late again, like every other night.

"I don't know why he always asks for our order," Kevin grumbled as he sat down in our pod. "It's the same every night."

Later that evening, around eight, long after we'd eaten our dinner, I walked over to get another slice of pepperoni to snack on while I was working. As I stepped up to the table where the pizza always sat, Kevin's words hit me.

Every night, we put together our pizza order for Donato's as if it were new. As if we'd order something different that evening. But we always ended up ordering the same thing. It just rebuilt itself every night: two pepperoni, two sausage, one veggie. We could have just put in a standing order at Donato's and achieved the same thing. It was the same pizza every night.

And it really was *every* night.

In fact, the table over by the whiteboard had taken on that distinctive "old pizza" aroma that lingered there, even during the day when the previous night's boxes had been cleared away.

When I think about it now, the whole office probably smelled like that, at least a little. It's gross to think about, but we ate while working all the time, and pizza grease was on our desks, our keyboards... everywhere. I probably was numb to it except by the table, where it was strongest.

It wasn't the mouth-watering smell of fresh pizza in a bustling, friendly pizzeria. It was the stale, lingering smell of months of old pizza.

And though I didn't think about it at the time, it was sort of symbolic. Though our office looked modern and had all the newest technology, underneath the modern appearance, we weren't modern at all. We were following the same stale, tired processes that would get us, our department, and our company nowhere.

The stale smell of old pizza was the smell of futility.

That was Part 1 of the lesson I was learning. It took a while longer for Part 2 to come around, but when it did, they both suddenly clapped together like two bookends on either side of a set of books I had been studying, almost without realizing it. And I saw what I'd been missing.

LIFE LESSON PART 2: ESCAPING HELL

Flash forward to a different job, where I worked with a different team, but one that had a lot of the same problems. Impossible-seeming goals, unavoidable obstacles, inevitable managerial miscommunications that created unnecessary setbacks... the list went on.

But by then, I had a potential way out.

One of my friends, Benjamin, was a programmer with the company where I worked as a project manager, and we used to go out a few times a week after work. I'm not sure which of us came up with the idea, but we were seriously thinking about starting our own business. I'd already been involved with one startup, which hadn't gone too far, though I'd learned a lot. So, I was game for the new venture.

We'd started brainstorming a few nights a week at the Brugge — a little bar in Broad Ripple, an eclectic little village inside Indianapolis.

One of our ideas hit for us as something we thought could work. We started really planning, and we pulled in a couple of other guys over the next few weeks. Finally, we got together in Benjamin's apartment and really started sketching out how we'd set up the company and start working on the product.

"All right," someone said. "Let's make our project plan."

Suddenly, everything screeched to a halt. I felt like I'd been punched in the gut, and everyone else had expressions that probably mirrored mine.

"No!" Benjamin protested. "That doesn't work."

I was shaking my head, too. "It's a death march," I remarked. The others echoed my statement.

"But then… how should we do it?" the first guy asked, perplexed.

We all began talking at once. What would we do if we didn't do things the same old way our big corporate companies did them?

Frankly, we couldn't afford to work like a big company anyway. Everything was on the line for us. We had to get a new product to market fast, we had to test it fast, and we had to improve and refine it fast. "Fast" was not in corporate vocabulary, except as a fantastic-seeming, unreachable goal they liked to dream about while shooting for "within three to five years." They could afford to take something to market years later. They had money to cushion themselves through that time.

But we didn't. We had no money coming in till we had a product and a customer.

So, our approach had to be the exact opposite of what a big company would do. And that's how we started designing our workflows.

There were four of us, each handling pieces of the work. I was the CEO, so I focused on the product pitch and figuring out how to raise some initial funding. The others handled code, architecture, data management, and other things. We talked to potential clients and learned what they wanted before we built the product. We kept these conversations ongoing so we could adjust our plan immediately when things weren't right. We got an initial product to the customer quickly and made improvements based on their comments.

We were up and running fast — not perfect, but good enough. Fast was more important than perfect. Perfection would come one step at a time as we improved things. But the truth was, it would also never come because the definition of "perfect" would keep changing as the customer's needs changed. We had to be OK with that, which was very different from how we had been conditioned to behave in our corporate lives.

As we were all working one evening to make the updates our customer had asked for, I suddenly realized how different this was from working for Steve.

That was when Part 2 of my lesson hit me.

There was no middle person between the team and the customer, like Steve had been at my first job. The team talked to the customer. We received information all at the same time. Together. We weren't playing telephone, depending on someone's interpretation.

As a result, communication issues were far fewer, and we could adjust much more quickly.

We were still working long hours, but now we were in the driver's seat. It wasn't the same. We were the ones making our own decisions and moving quickly to solve things right away instead of finding out about them, months or years after we should have.

We were doing everything differently, and it was working. This was the exact opposite of the way Steve had run the department I was in. And it was the best way we could have run ours. It wasn't exactly heaven, but it definitely wasn't hell.

Our little startup had solved all these problems just by… well, thinking like a startup. Using common sense. Not following the tried-and-true, traditional big-corporation practices.

Our small startup grew to employ a dozen people, and I learned a lot. We all did.

What we learned, in fact, was how to be Agile. And we did it not because someone told us to or because it was a "trend." We did it because it was natural. It was instinctive.

We didn't even *know* we were using Agile methods. We were just doing what made sense.

And that was the beginning.

BUSINESS AGILITY AS A MINDSET

Obviously, I eventually realized we were following Agile methods. When that startup fizzled because the idea didn't turn out to be viable long-term in the shifting market, we took what we learned to our next positions.

As I evolved in my career, taking on other contractor positions in large corporations, somehow, everything else I did always came back to Agile.

The reason is simple: Once you do it, you'll fight tooth and nail to not go back to those traditional ways that obviously don't work well when you're in a dynamic environment.

It's like riding a bicycle. Once you've learned to ride a bicycle, I dare you to try to fall off it. Yes, on purpose.

You can't. Your body doesn't want to fall over. It wants to stay upright and moving on the bike, not crashing to a halt and risking injury. Falling on purpose is just not natural.

When you're used to Agile methods, the other ways feel like you're literally trying to fail. You feel like you're trying to fall off your bicycle. It's unnatural. It totally goes against your instinct. You just can't force yourself to do it — and if you did, it would feel insane.

Project Brilliant

Eventually, my focus on business agility led me to several consulting engagements helping companies adopt methods that allowed them to operate more like the startup environment I'd experienced. When I formed my current company, Project Brilliant, it developed from an independent consultancy that really began in 2003, with Project Brilliant forming in 2011. As I began building my team, I also refined all the knowledge and techniques I had developed over my history of running startups and advising businesses in Agile methods.

Project Brilliant's purpose is simple: We're a business agility partner. We help bring businesses greater adaptability, speed, productivity, and customer satisfaction, among many other things.

You could say we help your business learn to ride a bicycle. After you learn, once you get past a certain point where we "let go," you'll keep going on your own. You won't want to stop riding. You definitely won't allow yourselves to fall over, let alone crash on purpose. The new way becomes the new natural. It makes sense, and it feels much better than the old way. Just think how much faster you can move on a bicycle than on foot.

Our team at Project Brilliant has helped many businesses transform their entire operations to not only meet their goals but also set them much higher than they could have imagined before. I'm not going to lie; it takes hard work. It's not a surface change; it's a deep change that requires leadership to think differently — to change the organization from the inside out.

The Benefits of Business Agility

But the transformation is worth it. If I told you I could help your teams increase their effectiveness (productivity, output, value delivery, etc.) by 10–15 percent, most CIOs would salivate uncontrollably. Well, what if I told you that our clients regularly experience a 300 percent increase — yes, that means triple — in their productivity and predictability, along with focusing on the right priorities?

"With your help, we've done in eight weeks what we couldn't do ourselves in six months," one of our recent clients told us. We hear similar comments often.

Our clients regularly experience a 300 percent increase — yes, that means triple — in their productivity and predictability.

And our clients don't just achieve their goals; they learn to choose the right goals — the ones that will result in longer-term impacts that allow them to sustain their momentum through volatile markets, shifting and adapting to fluid conditions and demands — with laser focus.

How do we do it? It's a set of techniques and a proven approach we've used in multiple organizations. While no two organizations are exactly the same, they often have many commonalities in their organizational design and operating models.

We helped our client shorten their timeframe from six months to eight weeks because we saw the whole picture.

Business agility starts with how we think about the interconnected nature of the organization as a complex, adaptive system. We know that the inner workings of the organization are bound by key aspects of its operating model, such as the structure, policies, and metrics that guide behaviors and decision-making. People within the organization function inside those boundaries as best they can, trying to achieve goals. With a focus on business agility, organizations seek to realign at a fundamental level in order to optimize their organizations — as a whole — to achieve shared goals that have overall business benefits and are typically externally facing, such as customer satisfaction.

We know the underlying root-cause problems and how to tackle them, rather than chasing surface-level issues or shiny objects. These may move the needle temporarily, but they don't have a real and lasting impact — and, in some cases, focusing on them may actually put you in an even worse position than before.

Getting enthusiastic about a silver-bullet solution that ends up not working is discouraging and frustrating. And it just doesn't have to happen.

In fact, I'd hate for it to happen to you, and that's one of the reasons I'm writing this book. I've helped a lot of people like you, in a lot of situations. I know that transforming your organization is possible because I've done it for others.

The first step is to identify and understand your real problem. You might think what you need to focus on is your processes, or your teamwork, or your productivity... but it's not. It's something far more difficult to change but more effective over the long term. Let's talk about it next.

CHAPTER 3

THE REAL PROBLEM

So, how have you been defining your problem? Did it show up on the list of the "usual" problems we looked at in Chapter 1 (team too slow, can't get things done, changing priorities, hampered by regulations, etc.)?

Maybe you see the problem as needing to be faster, leaner, or more efficient, or that you need skills training for your teams. Maybe you feel your team has morale issues or just needs to try harder.

I get it. Everyone wants simple, straightforward solutions. We all want the right checklist of steps to take to fix the situation. We want that one special formula that we can plug in, and it will just keep working forever. A silver bullet.

Does this sound like what you're looking for?

I know — it sounds great, doesn't it? If only we could find that easy, cross-it-off-the-list answer. By now you probably suspect that I have some bad news for you: You aren't going to get that kind of solution in this case because the main challenge is that you're looking for a simple solution to a complex problem.

The real problem is much larger and also much deeper, and it's not just one "thing" or group or situational facet but something that has been built into your whole organization from the beginning.

Your organization is perfectly designed to produce the results you're currently getting — failures and frustrations included. These stem from the culture that has been established over many years. What's acceptable, how we address problems, how we deal with people, how we evaluate priorities, and, most importantly, what we value are all aspects of our organizational culture.

> **Your organization is perfectly designed to produce the results you're currently getting — failures and frustrations included.**

Culture itself is multidimensional, but the most succinct description I've heard of organizational culture is: "Culture is what leadership will tolerate." It certainly starts with leadership, but it is a mindset that is pervasive throughout the whole organization. It's a set of expectations and assumptions that everyone in the organization has for themselves and each other. These expectations often hide underneath what everyone is saying and doing. The mindset doesn't necessarily exist in support of your stated goals, either. In fact, the results you're getting right now illustrate the mindset that's operating underneath your stated goals. The goals that are achieved are the ones the culture allows to be achieved.

The crazy thing is that your culture not only creates the problems you currently have, but it also creates the blind spot that's preventing you from seeing what's really wrong. All the things you feel you should be doing are probably contributing to and further exacerbating the problems you are currently facing. That's no one's "fault," including yours. But it's important to understand so you can start digging your way out of the tangle of challenges and find some real solutions to the deeper root causes.

Speaking of solutions — it's time to look in the mirror and get out of the comfort zone your current culture is creating for you — the same comfort zone that's keeping you from making progress.

That comfort zone is part of the real problem.

LET GO OF YOUR SECURITY BLANKET

Part of mainstream corporate culture revolves around the idea of having a set plan. For CIOs, this desire for stability often gets in the way of seeing and understanding the underlying problems.

CIOs have a tough set of challenges. You're constantly juggling issues related to risk, speed, efficiency, budget, quality, and team morale — and these can often compete for prioritization. When your department feels like it's constantly in reactive mode, trying to adjust to demands that can change overnight, the gut desire is naturally toward more control. After all, control feels like it leads to predictability, and predictability seems like the thing you need.

The problem is that trying to create more predictability through control actually creates a lot of other problems. When you lock in on a particular game plan or set of formulaic solutions, the world around you probably isn't going to follow your plan. When it doesn't, your plan will become obsolete — and quickly.

So, while you feel comfort that you have a plan, and that comfort is telling you things are OK, they really aren't. Your plan is a security blanket that makes you feel good, but it doesn't solve your real situation. When your world turns upside down, suddenly your plan doesn't make any sense. And your security blanket is gone.

What do you do then?

Easy. You make another plan, right?

You can see where this is going. It turns into a vicious cycle that doesn't get you where you need to go.

What if you had a different, more effective way to see and respond to the situation?

THE QUICK FIX VS. THE LIFESTYLE CHANGE

To solve the problems in your business, you have to get beyond the tactical "quick fix" focus and look at the business as a whole. The tactical solutions can actually make problems worse over time because they don't address the core needs underlying the whole situation.

For instance, say you're looking in the mirror, and you realize you've put on a few pounds. You could look at the situation in two ways.

You could think about the fact that your high school reunion is coming up in three months, and you want to lose the excess weight to look good and impress your former classmates. In this situation, you see your problem as mainly how you look, and how it will make you feel to look better for a group of people you want to impress.

Or, you could think about your weight gain as a way to start assessing your overall fitness level and habits. If you stay on this path, you'll keep gaining weight and eventually be at risk of heart disease or other health issues. In this situation, you see your problem as a holistic quality of life issue that could affect everything, both for you and for your loved ones.

If you're the first person, you'll go on a diet, lose the weight for the reunion, and then probably go back to your old habits afterward (maybe until the next reunion). You aren't likely to keep the weight off because your goal was just to lose it for a short time. You've solved your immediate "problem." But you haven't necessarily fixed any health issues or made your life better in the long run.

But if you're the second person, you're never going to eat french fries again, and you're going to change your exercise habits and make a lot of other shifts because you've seen your problem as something much bigger and more complex than one small goal can fix. It's not a *goal*. You're willing to make a total lifestyle change to live a longer and healthier life for another twenty-five, thirty, even fifty years.

These situations show a huge difference in approach — not just in how you're looking at the goals but also in your commitment to achieving them.

Creating sustainable change in your business requires the second approach. You have to realize it's a lifestyle change. It's not just about achieving one small goal and being finished. And it's also not about targeting only one aspect of the situation or organization.

While you may be looking at one facet — your team, specific individuals, the market, your leadership, whatever — as the "problem," the fact is, there's probably a whole set of underlying cultural factors creating the situation — even within yourself. Your organization is designed with these inherent problems embedded within its functions.

WHY PEOPLE MISS THE PROBLEM

Please don't think I'm criticizing you here. I'm really not. This is a mind shift pretty much everyone has to make at first. We're just not taught to think in this new way. We're relying on mainstream corporate thinking — and it is that type of thinking that needs to change.

I'm not saying the type of thinking taught at all the business schools doesn't work. It does work for running efficiently in a status-quo environment. When you take these methods further, especially in a dynamic, rapidly changing environment, they stop working and can become serious obstacles.

Think about some of the methods you're taught. Lean, for instance, is one of the gold standards of corporate measurement. "Are we lean enough?" "How can we get leaner?" These are the questions we ask ourselves.

But is getting leaner always the solution?

I like to use sports to explain some of these business concepts. If you think about lean in terms of types of athletes, to me, a good analogy is a marathon runner. Those people have to be super tight, super skinny, and as light as possible because they've got to run twenty-something miles. To be as efficient as possible, they get into a rhythm with the same motion in every stride. They're trying to use their energy to their best ability, but it's essentially all in a straight line.

Companies do the same kind of thing. They lean themselves down to the point where they're not really able to do anything else. They've made themselves so efficiently lean, to the best of their ability, that when a bump in the road comes up, they struggle to deal with it and recover their stride. All they know is how to be lean and run in a straight line and be as light as possible.

It's like the comfortable plan we don't want to relinquish. It seems like we're making progress, but if we've created a team full of marathon runners, what happens when something changes? They are tooled to do their one thing well. Now they have to totally retool to respond — and they aren't very quick at doing it.

Is there a better goal to shoot for in terms of more responsiveness to the market and other changing situations?

Keeping with the sports metaphor, when I ask people to think of a more agile kind of athlete, they often bring up a gymnast, who has to do floor exercise or balance beam or fly around on the bars. That is definitely more agile than a marathon runner because gymnastics is more about being able to pivot and switch directions, do flips, and maintain balance no matter what position gymnasts find themselves in. However, that situation doesn't apply much to business. Gymnastics is a sport where an individual is the only one on the floor at any given time. Business, on the other hand, is not an individual activity. It requires a team. Therefore, we need to find a better metaphor.

The analogy I find most fitting, and not just because I live in Indiana, is basketball. In basketball, everyone on the team has to run, jump, pass, play defense, sprint back and forth, shoot, steal the ball, and make layups. It's high-scoring, fast-paced, exciting, and represents so many Agile concepts! So, we could say that a team goal for agility is to be more like a basketball team than a marathon runner. You probably can't take a marathon runner straight from that sport, put them on a basketball team, and expect them to be a good basketball player. They may be excellent athletes — but they're specifically targeted toward a particular goal. They haven't trained for quick response or for passing a ball or for doing layups. No matter how fit they are, they'll still need time to adjust.

Another similar mindset is risk management. When you're so focused on risk that you don't want to take any chances, you stick with the comfortable "tried-and-true" tactics that also don't work. Change involves risk and unpredictability. Without allowing those things, you can't really make meaningful change.

The key is realizing that the problem you've been trained to solve — the one you're also training your team to solve — is really a symptom of a much deeper issue in need of attention. To understand it, you have to step much further back and look at the broader situation and the larger organization.

IT'S TIME FOR A CULTURE SHIFT

So. You're probably wondering, how do you know when all those traditional methods that you are so comfortable with are actually not helpful? Should you just toss everything out and start over? How do you measure when lean is too lean, or risk management is too oppressive, or whatever other method you're using has gone beyond the point of helping you?

Well, you ask questions a startup would ask.

You make assumptions as if you're a startup trying to experiment toward a "good enough" result that you can learn from each time.

You look at your business completely differently, with completely different assumptions and expectations than you have today.

If your team isn't able to adapt to change quickly, it's probably set up too rigidly, and it's time for a change. If their productivity isn't what you want it to be, it's time to look at what's in their way. If you feel their morale is low, it's time to step back and look at the complexities bringing about that situation.

The key is to understand how to adapt and respond quickly to meet the demands of the market.

This is what business agility means in the twenty-first century. It's about retooling your organization to respond nimbly to new demands, the way a startup would, without the baggage that's holding you back.

You're probably mentally looking at me like I'm nuts right now. "But Aaron, startups are small and fast, and they can turn on a dime," you want to say. "How the hell can my organization, which has been in business for X number of years, with all the hierarchical obstacles and bureaucracy and politics that go along with that, possibly operate like a startup? I can't even imagine what that would look like!"

I didn't say it was quick and easy. But just because it's going to take time and effort, doesn't mean it isn't the right decision.

And actually, once you understand how it works, it isn't as difficult as you'd think. Yes, it does require commitment and time, of course. I'm not going to make false promises or let you off the hook there. But if you're all-in on the reasoning behind the shift and the gains to be had from making it, you'll feel like it's worth the time and effort. And once you get there, as I said before, you will never want to go back.

It requires transforming every aspect of your business — including your goals. Obviously, that means involving more than your own department. You'll have to put yourself out there, make allies, and set a vision for the future that others will want to follow. But if you do it right, it will lead to amazing things for your business.

I realize you probably have a ton of questions flying around in your head right now, and I'm going to try to answer all of them in the coming chapters. Stick with me — you'll start seeing how this might shape out for you. And if you're already convinced, you'll also get a roadmap for how to get there without banging your head against the wall too much.

All right: Let's start turning your marathon runners into a championship basketball team.

UNLOCKING MOMENTUM – THE KEYS

CHAPTER 4

A NEW VISION

REEXAMINE YOUR STARTING POINT

To plot how to get from Point A to Point B on your GPS, you need to know where Point A actually is — in other words, where you're starting from. Otherwise, it's hard to set a course. It's basically the same with setting a new vision for your organization or department. To do that, you need to first look at your current reality.

You've already realized that your current situation isn't desirable, and we've already talked about how none of the go-to solutions have worked. Let's take a moment to examine why.

Your organization, like most, probably does the typical balancing act: setting ambitious goals and mitigating potential failure to reach those goals in the face of so many things you really cannot control, no matter how hard you try.

You may dutifully take up your own responsibilities to achieve them as part of the team, and you may do your best to make everything happen... but you may also wonder sometimes why it has to be so hard. If you're at least somewhat of a realist, you understand that the stated goals and the desired metrics are only part of the whole situation. There are the expectations, and then there are the harsh realities. And the realities make the whole situation a lot more challenging than anyone wants to admit sometimes — maybe a lot of the time.

In terms of realities and experience, for instance, you know which KPIs senior leadership wants to see from your department, but you also know, based on past experience, you're probably not going to achieve all of them exactly as desired. You may even capture your own additional data as a defense to ensure you can explain why you didn't meet the goals if that should happen. CYA (cover your a**) is a learned behavior in many organizations as a survival mechanism for many CIOs.

You know that when you set your project timelines, due to unforeseen factors, they will probably change — in fact, it's not uncommon for them to expand out by 100–200 percent, resulting in years longer than the original plan. So, when you start with Plan A, in the back of your mind, you're also resigned to the fact that Plan A will probably end up evolving toward Plan D or Plan E or something even further down the alphabet (and also further into the calendar). That's just how things work. You're in an organization where you have to rely on a sequence of events and dependencies on others, and their priorities don't always line up with yours. They have other competing demands, whether or not they wish it were otherwise.

You know that IT is often viewed as a "necessary evil," a cost center, and as CIO, you're in danger of being seen as a gatekeeper who's slowing business decisions and hampering opportunity. That means you'll have to continually sell yourself and your team as eager order-takers and problem-solvers focused on efficiently addressing unspoken needs. Yet you'll also have to continue managing risk, team workload, morale, and all your other responsibilities that might create the very friction or delays your business partners complain about.

You realize that the sprawling jungle of internal IT and other corporate policies and processes create snares and obstacles that will entangle projects in their tendrils, keeping anyone from getting anywhere quickly. This is especially true if you're in a heavily regulated industry. Yet, you also have to accept that no one has time to take a machete to the jungle — or even think about it — because they're all too busy putting out the next set of fires in the village down the trail.

I could go on, but I'm hoping you get my point and can relate to this kind of picture. This is your reality — every day.

Figure 4.1 The Rube Goldberg Machine

A Rube Goldberg machine, named after the famed engineer/cartoonist Rube Goldberg, is set up to be as complex and inefficient as possible in carrying out a simple task.[1]

In fact, the typical traditional corporate IT organization is kind of like a Rube Goldberg machine. Logically, it should be obvious that you can't put things into this machine and expect them to come out great. But that's exactly what companies do every day because they're not looking at the whole machine. They're mainly looking at their individual parts and trying to make them work. Just like everyone else, you're expected to navigate your projects through this convoluted machine, keep your cool, help meet the next set of business goals, and make sure everyone else is happy.

And maybe you're doing all of that — but at what price? Your sanity? Your physical health? Your team morale? Your own morale? Do you feel tired, frustrated, and overwhelmed? And if so, is it any wonder?

I've got a better idea. Let's start to disassemble this crazy machine and put a new one together — one that makes better sense. One that is set up to achieve the goals. One that operates on the principles of business agility.

WHAT IS BUSINESS AGILITY?

What, exactly, do I mean by business agility?

The term reflects the ability of an organization to fluidly adapt to market change as a unified, cohesive entity while continuously delivering value to its customers. It refers to an organization's ability to:

- adapt quickly to market changes,
- deliver value early and often,

- innovate, and
- remain flexible in response to customer demands and emerging trends.

This concept encompasses not just timeliness but also the ability to pivot and adjust strategically as situations evolve. In a fast-paced business environment, agility ensures that a company can respond swiftly to new opportunities, changes in consumer preferences, and disruptions caused by technological advancements or global events. It involves not just leadership but every level of the organization, from decision-makers to delivery teams.

The Business Agility Institute measures business agility as behaviors within five "domains"[2]:

- Responsive customer-centricity
- Engaged culture
- Value-based delivery
- Flexible operations
- People-first leadership

Note that the only one that doesn't revolve around people in some way, directly or peripherally, is "flexible operations." Business agility centers on people because it relies on everyone in the organization to make key decisions — not just the senior leadership. It's this characteristic that enables the flexible operations the business needs for adaptiveness.

A Foundation Based on Agile

Let's also take a look at the term Agile as a root concept of business agility. There are a lot of definitions of Agile out there, but to me, Agile is a mindset of iterative and incremental delivery of value through collaboration and continuous improvement.

That's a concise sentence with a lot baked into it. Let's dissect it for a moment.

- **Mindset** — a way of thinking
- **Iterative** — repeated attempts
- **Incremental** — piece by piece
- **Delivery** — getting it to the user
- **Value** — something usable and useful
- **Collaboration** — working together with others, such as internal team members, stakeholders, and external customers
- **Continuous improvement** — always looking for ways to make things better, including the product, people, ways of working, etc.

When we at Project Brilliant work with our clients, we apply Agile methods to the entire organization, using proven techniques to holistically transform it over time.

Principles of Business Agility

Agile was originally created to transform the world of software development. However, its principles also apply to business in general and, thus, organizations as a whole. Therefore, at Project Brilliant, we follow a set of principles for business agility based on the guidelines outlined in the original *Agile Manifesto.*[3]

We can summarize those principles with some concise interpretations:

1. Satisfy the customer continuously
2. Welcome change
3. Deliver early and often
4. Business + developers collaborate daily
5. Leaders trust and support the team
6. Co-locate — use face-to-face communication
7. Getting to done = progress
8. Work at a sustainable pace
9. Maintain high quality — no cutting corners
10. Keep it simple
11. Self-organizing teams know best
12. Improve continuously

I'll go into more detail on these in later chapters, but for now, let's use the list as a reference for the next part of this chapter.

HOW DO YOU RATE?

Let's do a rough evaluation of your own organization. Think of a scale of 1 to 5, in which the following values apply:

1 = Never/Not at all
2 = Sometimes
3 = Halfway
4 = Mostly
5 = Always/Completely

Rate yourself in each of the above twelve principles. Write down your answers on a separate sheet of paper.

Now think about this: What are your biggest problems right now? What keeps you up at night? How do these problems relate to those twelve principles?

You can also apply the same questions/ratings to your company as a whole. How do those answers differ from the ones about your department? It can be an interesting comparison that gives insights into some of the external things holding you back.

WHAT'S THE IDEAL SITUATION?

After you've rated your department using the principles above, start thinking about what the ideal picture would look like in relationship to each of them. For instance, if you satisfied your customer continuously, what would that look like? Jot your answers down. Your department may have both internal and external customers, so this may be a more complex question than one might think.

How would it feel to "welcome change"? For instance, suppose your business partner comes to you and says what they thought they needed two months ago doesn't make sense anymore, and they want to do something completely different. You're halfway through building the previous solution. Would you welcome the change request? What would your mindset be? What would have to be in place for you to feel positive about it, at least in some measure?

Look especially at the things you rated lowest for your department and see which ones line up with the majority of your headaches. If you fixed these, what would your organization be able to do that it can't do now? How would you be seen in the organization? What would people do differently when they interact with you and your team?

Maybe these questions are too abstract to answer with much specific detail right now, but do you have at least a glimmer of an idea that things could evolve if you implemented some changes?

It may seem daunting — even impossible — at this moment. But I know for a fact that it isn't. And a lot of clients who felt exactly as you do now have proved that it isn't impossible.

SHIFTING GEARS IN THE BACK OFFICE

Remember my friend Perry? When he came to me, he was about to kick off a system retirement and data migration project involving a new back-office program. As we got more deeply involved in the initiative, I saw that he faced a number of challenges: Perry's industry is highly regulated, and he also had the outsourced delivery team in India to deal with — or not. There was limited trust between the teams and leadership, and as he mentioned, many of his peers or others who would be leading teams were new in their positions.

To add more pressure to the situation, failures were not acceptable in the organization. If the retirement of this large system wasn't a success, it would also be seen as a lack of success for Agile methods as a whole. In addition, Perry and his Change Leadership Team (CLT) had other challenges — while they had committed to their approach to Agile, the rest of the organization hadn't yet. So, the members of the CLT still had several competing priorities and other responsibilities preventing them from each personally going all-in. This impacted their availability for even simple things like having a consistently attended daily standup meeting. Being pulled into some other issue or random "high priority" meeting at the last minute was common, especially early on.

However, through a thoughtfully designed and very Agile implementation, the teams reached their desired outcomes, becoming more predictable and consistently completing their Sprint commitments. Releases became more frequent — every two to four weeks rather than once or twice a year. The company decided to continue working with the offshore teams in India, so the CLT agreed to provide them with in-person team coaching as well, bringing them into better understanding and alignment with the local teams.

The result of the new approach was that Perry's group took on a large-scale initiative originally slated for three years (and realistically predicted at closer to five years) and accomplished all the high-priority "must-have" work in just two years. This allowed them to make the cutover and turn off the old system (and save the cost of another year of licensing fees). It was a HUGE win, and not only saved them several million in real dollar costs, but the time savings also allowed them to move up several other major initiatives and get them started and finished years sooner as well!

It's no surprise that the rest of the organization took notice. Soon, Perry was getting a lot

The result of the new approach was that Perry's group took on a large-scale initiative originally slated for three years (and realistically predicted at closer to five years) and accomplished all the high-priority "must-have" work in just two years.

of attention, in a good way. He was getting inquiries from all over the business to share his approach. Everyone wanted to get on the bandwagon of success and started trying to figure out how they could do what he did in their area.

First, it was customer support, then product management, then finance, and even legal over the course of time. If you think of this Agile approach in terms of principles and a mindset shift, the applicability is really quite broad. Every area of the organization dealing with complex outcomes can benefit in big and meaningful ways.

The only reason they don't do it more often is that figuring out how is not always obvious or straightforward, and they may already have assumptions that don't necessarily apply.

COMMON OBJECTIONS

Leading any change can be challenging due to people's resistance to change in general. You'll meet with skepticism in any new endeavor, and that's not a bad thing. In fact, it's usually best to nail down the main objections right up front — including your own — so you can see how to address them. Otherwise, they'll hide under the surface, hampering your efforts.

Here are some objections we commonly encounter.

"That may have worked for this one company, but I have a different experience."

Most people in IT have at least some exposure to Agile and have read the text of the principles. But putting principles into practice sometimes doesn't go as you predict.

It can be frustrating to have someone offering a solution that seems like it doesn't apply. However, what didn't work before may have been related to so many variables that it's tough to just dismiss it out of hand. Even if you've been in several different situations where Agile "didn't work," there could be many perfectly valid reasons that have nothing to do with whether or not it's a good strategy.

Jean Tabaka lists a whole slew of ways Agile might not work, and these have more to do with implementation or other considerations.[4] For instance, it could have been as simple as not having the right people in the planning meetings or the company just giving up too early. Maybe the culture didn't support the new effort. Dismissing it upfront without doing the work of supporting the transformation can lead to missed opportunities.

"OK, that might be good in my own department, but I can't do that with my whole organization."

I get it; you're the CIO. You don't have the authority to just start telling your business peers what to do.

The great thing is that you don't need to. Usually, what happens in the case of a successful initial implementation is that the leaders of the other units start to see what's happening, and they get curious. Eventually, they want to get in on it, too. They can see how the changes have benefited the first few groups. Then, it's just a matter of expanding the template to work in other areas/situations, learning and adapting as you go. That's not necessarily up to you, though. So, of course, you'd want to collaborate to help them find the tangible ways it can apply, and how they can prove it through data and metrics.

"How do I know the ROI will be worth the cost? I don't want to take that risk."

When you follow the methods Project Brilliant uses, you usually start small and test things before you expand to larger situations. This helps manage early risk.

Another great idea from Perry's team is to balance the cost against the ROI. That was one important goal they set: the benefit of Agile must outweigh the related costs. The "early and often" deliveries and engagement across the business allowed them to show progress and actively navigate the course hand-in-hand with their stakeholders.

It was clear to everyone as they went along that things were getting done sooner — and better — than ever before. Not only did it feel good, but they could quantify the results based on their initial expected three-year (and assumed five-year) timeline. They then used this data to make further decisions on how to expand Agile in the following years. You could easily do the same.

"The chaos and headaches are not worth the benefits."

This one cracks me up. Go back and look at that Rube Goldberg illustration again. How is that not a picture of chaos and headaches?

What this is really about is the chaos and headaches you *know and are familiar with*, versus the ones you don't. The unknown is scary — it's hard to manage risk in the unknown. However, are you really managing risk by not changing, or are you clinging to a security blanket of denial?

What are you really controlling by not changing? What's the opportunity cost of not changing? You have the same comfortably predictable internal chaos and headaches, but you're not in control of the market or your competitors' decisions. If your competitors are getting ahead because they're willing to take a risk and you're not, then not taking a risk, in effect, becomes a bigger risk.

What this is really about is the chaos and headaches you *know and are familiar with*, versus the ones you don't.

I'm not trying to be facetious here. I'm just stating the obvious issue that is often hard to face. We can't escape change. We may as well start welcoming it, especially when it can benefit us. Even if it's hard and uncomfortable, it's usually the right thing to do.

"I don't want to put my neck on the line with senior leadership."

I understand this fear. I can't give you a guarantee that trying to achieve business agility won't create tension between you and your leadership. I certainly can't guarantee that you'll succeed, either. There's never a guarantee when you're in a complex environment.

However, there's definitely a lot to gain by being willing to try something new. And there are ways to do it that aren't as risky. For instance, you can take a conservative approach that proves itself as it goes. Your leadership will see how it works over time, and the facts will speak for themselves.

It's about adopting an attitude of small experiments. They lead to more knowledge, which leads to less failure. Wouldn't you rather fail in a small way and adjust than bite off more than you can chew and end up choking?

"My organization is too big to operate like a startup."

This may be surprising, but the main issue with business agility isn't about size. It's about structure. It actually doesn't really matter how big a company is if its structure supports delivering value to its customers. Structural and cultural issues go hand in hand, and they can be fixed through smart alignment strategies with a focus on the long term. If a large, sprawling organization like Capital One can implement business agility methods, I'm guessing your company can, too.

WHAT IT TAKES: A MULTIFACETED APPROACH

As I've mentioned before, creating lasting change involves more than simply fixing a superficial problem or trying to change a single element at the expense of all others. That's why Project Brilliant's framework for retooling an organization for better agility, AgileOS®, starts with a three-pronged approach that looks at the most important facets to create change: Leaders, Products, and Teams.

Figure 4.2: The AgileOS® Framework

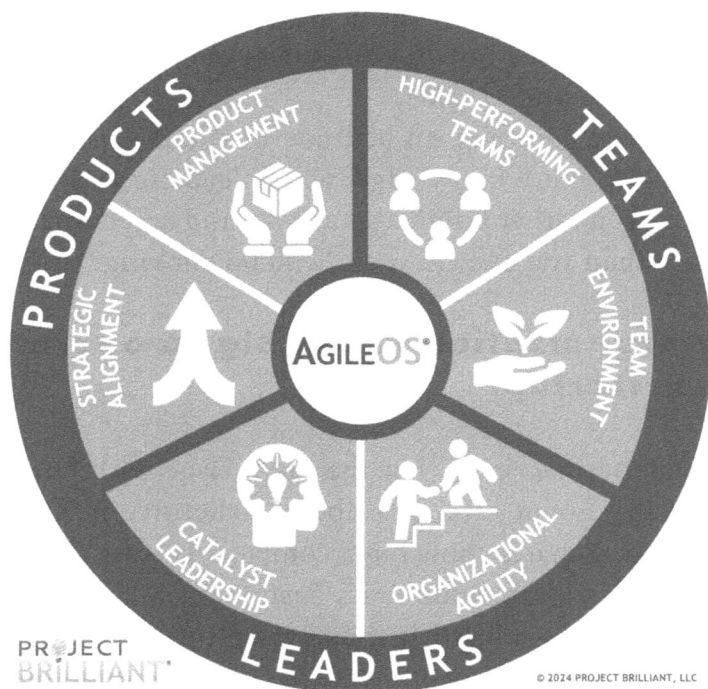

Project Brilliant developed its AgileOS® framework as a multidimensional approach to handling business agility transformations throughout entire organizations.

We start with the Leaders, then move to address the Products (vs. projects), and finally, we focus on the Teams themselves. There's a lot of thinking behind this model, and the sequence is also important. I'll go into those things in the coming chapters, where we'll explore each of these facets in more depth.

CHAPTER 5

BUILDING AGILE LEADERS

In discussing business agility or Agile conversions in general, you'll hear of different strategies focused on top-down or bottom-up approaches, or a combination of both. Every organization is different, and some things work better in one than they may in others. But as a rule, if leadership isn't ~~onboard with~~ *actively leading* the changes required, the transformation probably won't succeed.

Yes, that strikethrough and italic are intentional. It's not about passively "being onboard." It's about being completely committed and actively involved in leading the change. The change *starts* with leadership — in both mindset and activity. That's why the "Building Agile Leaders" chapter comes first.

In fact, the Business Agility Institute (BAI) has confirmed that transformations reach significantly higher maturity when led from the C-suite or board of directors than when led from the line of business leaders, with an average maturity score of 5.8 (out of 10) for the board, 5.4 for the C-level, and 4.1 for the line of business leaders.[5]

Perhaps not surprisingly, BAI also found that of all challenges in achieving business agility, the number one challenge companies reported was ineffective leadership, followed by poor change leadership at number two. These ranked well above mindset (no. 3), unsuitable practices and processes (no. 4), and unsuitable organizational structure (no. 5).[6]

"Leaders set the tone for the entire organization," the report stated. "Yet, leaders continue to use legacy leadership behaviors which are not aligned to the desired organizational culture and send mixed messages to staff."[7] Their recommendation? Educate leaders in leading complex change and setting realistic expectations.

The number one challenge companies reported was ineffective leadership, followed by poor change leadership at number two.

That's why I can't stress this enough: As the leader carrying the flag for this change, you're enormously important. The interesting fact is that you're important in ways you may not yet be aware of, for doing things you're not yet used to doing.

This change will fundamentally transform not only your whole organization but how you and the rest of your leadership team function within that organization. Without those two changes happening concurrently, your chances of succeeding decrease significantly. That means the more aware you are of what will happen during this transformation, the better prepared you'll be.

It helps to have an idea of how and why we got where we are today so we can start framing the right map for the future.

AN EVOLUTION OF MANAGEMENT MINDSET IN THE US

Today's management and leadership values didn't spring out of nowhere. They evolved in a natural way to adapt to changing conditions and demands. That's important to note when considering how things are changing today.

At the beginning of the Industrial Revolution, most management focused on manual labor, such as workers in early industrial factories like steel mills, oil refineries, and early manufacturing plants. As people in search of better economic circumstances moved from farms into cities, these inexperienced and undereducated workers needed direct instruction on how to do the tasks expected of them. Then Frederick Winslow Taylor came along and started working on ways companies could become more efficient in their approach. He eventually developed the concept of scientific management, which focused on measuring activity as a means to develop standards of efficiency that management could use to benchmark expectations.[8]

The center of authority in that situation sat with the numbers and direct capability of the manager to provide oversight and on-the-spot instruction and correction. Management theorized that the more efficient the labor became, the more competitive the company could be in the market. The result was a top-down, command-control style in which management set expectations, and workers were required to meet them through long hours and often intense working conditions. Incentives were introduced to encourage better performance; if someone could create more than the required number of products in the measured time, they may earn more pay. Meanwhile, if you didn't meet the benchmark, you were likely at risk of being replaced by someone who could.

All of this made sense during that time, when the bulk of the work focused largely on manual production efforts heavily reliant on a series of individual activities that could be readily understood and directly managed. Those companies that used Taylor's methods to gain efficiency and higher levels of production saw more profits than those who didn't. Profit, therefore, naturally encouraged the ongoing use of the systems that increased it.

But then, as it tends to do, the world changed. Beginning in 1946, W. Edwards Deming, an engineer turned physicist turned quality control expert, was invited to Japan through the US government to help rebuild the industrial capability of our former foe.[9]

He became a frequent visitor, and his influence transformed Japan's entire manufacturing process. Ironically, he was barely known in the US at the time. Yet the Japanese became so successful at using his methods that the US eventually "imported" many of them from the Japanese. Among his principles was the idea of putting more power into the hands of those closest to the work of building the products, allowing them to take more responsibility for monitoring quality during active production.[10]

This development required management to put more trust in their employees through the implementation of Lean principles and practices. More complicated sets of organizational roles began to expand as companies continued to adapt and fulfill the new requirements. Line workers now became specialists in their area of production, understanding better than anyone — even better than the managers — what quality looked like and how to spot defects. This trust resulted in giving authority to the worker to go so far as to stop the entire assembly line if they spotted a significant defect. The idea was to fix an issue in real-time and stop it from recurring.

This again shifted the role of management. Instead of measuring and directly controlling the movement and activity of each worker, managers could now trust the local experts to be masters of their stations on the assembly line. Managers could take a broader view and monitor the output of the entire line, focusing on the overall line's output and quality metrics. This is an entirely different approach than individual task management, focusing on the input of labor. We've successfully shifted management's attention from inputs to outputs.

Then, toward the end of the twentieth century, into the 2000s, and continuing now, the advancement of customer expectations and technology have rapidly increased the speed and complexity of market needs. Highly customized products and solutions delivered in near-real-time are required to keep up with today's needs.

In response, the work expanded to include more abstract, knowledge-focused areas rather than merely doing concrete tasks producing tangible products. Multiple knowledge and execution areas must be brought together quickly in order to respond in a timely manner. We can no longer wait in the long cycles of planning and serialized sequences of stage-gate work approvals. Automation has begun to fill roles that humans once occupied. Empowered teams of people must make real-time decisions before the window of opportunity passes them, and the company, by.

In this new environment, it is nearly impossible for management to make decisions in the way they had fifty years ago. Things simply move too fast. Often, the managers can't understand the moving parts well enough to make a fast decision. Other times, by the time they reach a conclusion, everything will change again, making the decision obsolete before the workers are able to execute it.

These challenges force managers to take a different approach. Instead of trying to control the situation and push everything up the leadership chain of command for decisions, they empower teams to make their own decisions on the fly. Management becomes less involved in the daily work and more involved in setting up their teams for success.

For this to work, managers must take on a new responsibility. Instead of managing the workers, or even the work, they must focus on the environment in which the workers do their work. The more they can create optimal conditions, provide tools and information, and delegate decision-making authority, the more effectively their teams can operate and create successful outcomes.

Managers have shifted from managing activity and inputs to managing higher-level outputs to now managing outcomes. Management has moved from measuring how many hours a day people work, beyond how many cars were produced and defects discovered, to now focusing on "are our teams even creating the right product for the right customer, and is this the right time to do so?" This is the evolution of management in companies and is modern leadership in action.

HOW THE RUBE GOLDBERG MACHINE CAME TO BE

No one understood the IT Rube Goldberg machine better than my uncle Frank.

Frank, my dad's older brother, ended up being one of the most tech-savvy guys of his time. When computers initially came on the market for general use, he was the first guy in his organization to get one. His boss wasn't even sure what they were going to use it for, but he assumed Frank would come up with something.

Frank was kind of a coffee nut. At home or at work, he inevitably had a giant mug of coffee in hand. So, it figures that he learned about his first opportunity when he was in the breakroom getting a coffee refill. One of the business-side folks, Ron, happened to come in just as Frank was setting the pot down and heading back to his office to continue learning how to program the computer.

"Hi, Frank," Ron said. "How's it going?"

"It's great!" Frank said. "I just got a computer, and I've been programming it to do all kinds of stuff. Right now, I'm trying to figure out how to use it to solve business problems."

"What kind of problems?" Ron asked, puzzled. He was sort of intrigued, but he really needed to get back to his office and help his secretary put the stuff together for their biweekly project list.

Frank said, "Tell me some of the stuff that you're working on, and I'll see what I can do to help you."

They started brainstorming. After a few minutes, with some more prompts from Frank, Ron thought of that darn list his secretary was putting together. "My boss wants me to keep track of all the people who are involved in this big project we're doing," Ron said. "I have to send him a list every couple of weeks. My secretary has to type it all up every time, even though we just have to add and subtract a couple of names."

Frank's eyes lit up. "That should be easy!" he said. "If you give me their names and what to add and take off each week, I can keep track of that for you."

With Ron's list, Frank put the information into a data file, printed the list out with his flashy dot matrix printer (hey, it was the '90s), and gave it to Ron.

Ron was stunned. He could get a biweekly list, in alphabetical order, just by giving Frank a couple of pieces of information each week?

"What else can you do?" Ron asked, excited now.

This probably sounds hilariously rudimentary if you weren't around back then, but this was how things evolved. Ron and Frank started a productive collaboration in which, every few days, Ron brought something new that he wanted to implement, and Frank gathered all the parameters and brought back the finished product. Soon, other people started making requests, too, and Frank solved their problems with equal success.

The other folks were thrilled with the help, and Frank loved knowing he could make their jobs easier. Everyone was happy.

Then, someone said, "Hey, it's really good that you can do all this technology stuff for us. Why don't we have someone else start making a list of the requests, so you can focus on doing the technical work? That will be much more efficient."

The new paradigm added challenges. No longer talking directly to the person with the problem, Frank was now talking to the person in the middle. Sometimes, the requests didn't make sense, and the intermediary didn't seem to be able to answer the questions — or their answers turned out to be wrong. Plus, the number of middlepersons just seemed to keep growing as the number of requests grew. Eventually, strict processes on both sides made it even more cumbersome to get anything done.

Now, no one was happy. Frank didn't know if what he was doing was helping, and even if it wasn't, he couldn't fix the problem quickly. Meanwhile, the others didn't know why Frank couldn't get solutions to them sooner. The whole situation was frustrating. Soon, people dreaded asking IT to do anything. It would always take twice as long to get done as it should, and it would never work like they wanted.

This was the start of waterfall project management. It's how the Rube Goldberg device got built — by trying to make the IT guy efficient.

Efficient Inefficiency

Command-control organizations often adopt centralized decision-making structures that ensure consistency in governing the organization. Consistency is that comfy security blanket we talked about earlier.

These structures form the internal policy framework, which in turn creates all its standard operating procedures as well as the informal work processes and culture. This internal set of "laws" by which the organization functions, along with all the internal structures that monitor/enforce them, inevitably forms the company bureaucracy.

Bureaucracy is helpful in ensuring consistency, but it can often conflict with innovation and change. We've all run into the "this is our policy" brick wall that cuts off innovation before it can even begin, or the "this is how it's always been done" mindset that isn't allowed to adapt to address evolving stakeholder needs.

The bureaucracy was created in response to a problem — likely one that occurred long ago, in a galaxy far, far away. The whole situation may have changed and adapted, but the bureaucracy can be an immovable stalwart. It's set up to support a marathon-runner style — just keep doing the same thing in the same direction. It wasn't designed to adapt quickly to new situations because that was never its purpose.

As a result, the organization is haunted by the ghosts of past decisions and priorities. The success metrics and KPIs we were using three, five, or even ten years ago are still around, but many are possibly no longer relevant.

And since management's main responsibility centers on their own department, they focus on getting better and better at their own version of marathon running, whether or not it helps — or even hampers — the overall organization in reaching its larger goals. Large-scale inefficiencies, therefore, abound, even when the picture looks good within the departments themselves.

Think of it this way: In our Rube Goldberg machine example, our department is responsible for a boot-on-a-stick pendulum. A marble comes from somewhere else and activates the boot. When it swings, it kicks over the cup that holds a new marble, which rolls down a ramp to collide with and spring a mousetrap that springs and releases a helium-filled balloon whose string pulls open a hamster cage door. Man, we're really good at that, and we've made that process super-efficient!

Now, suppose there are twenty other groups in the organization doing something similar for their piece of the overall puzzle. Finally, the end contraption pushes a lever down on the toaster to produce toasted bread for the customer. Each sub-machine is cutting-edge efficient, down to the nanosecond. In total, there may be 300 steps in the overall machine, and each sub-machine is as efficient at its steps as it can be.

But what if we only need four or five of the 300 steps to deliver real customer value? While we might be efficient at getting that marble from the cup to the mousetrap, at the end of the day, no one needs that mousetrap to spring. It's just something we've always done, and at this point, it's just for show.

That's a kick in the gut. And yet, if we're not looking at the whole complex structure, it doesn't matter how well each subsection is tuned. The overall system itself isn't set up for efficiency. It is possible to be efficiently inefficient. To me, that's a good description of a Rube Goldberg machine. And it's probably a description of most corporate IT organizations in the world today.

Role Conflicts

Something obviously has to give. The first thing we need to look at is why it hasn't.

One of the aspects is the structure. Leaders see their existence as being tied to their particular "submachine," which is typically a functional area. That area has been seen as important in the current mindset. But if it centers on one of the unnecessary steps in the Rube Goldberg machine, what then? Will they be let go? Reorganized? I don't blame leaders and managers for not wanting to redefine themselves out of a job. Who would?

Nobody wants to work in an unnecessary submachine, but they may not see a way out. "Most leaders aren't fighting Agile," wrote Darrell Rigy, Sarah Elk, and Steve Berez in *Harvard Business Review*. "They simply haven't understood how it applies to their roles or how to perform those roles in ways that enhance agility."[11]

The key is to see an alternative — not an ending. The alternative doesn't have to be threatening. It's actually a much better scenario for everyone — the leaders and the team alike. The first thing is to start getting leadership and management to see possibilities for change that enable more opportunities, instead of just taking away the current comfort zone.

EMBRACE THE COUNTERINTUITIVE

One of the first things we do when we're working with an organization is to start helping leadership become open to those new possibilities — and this requires having an open mind.

You may have deduced by now that, as part of the transformation to Agile organizations, the models we teach leaders often seem counterintuitive. As I've mentioned, managers like the idea of having control, but we ask them to reevaluate the idea of control. In most cases, they don't really have control anyway; what they have is just a perception of control.

Giving up the current business organizational model can feel threatening without a clear path forward, so we need a new idea upon which leaders can hang their hats. But it is often understood that in a complex environment, the twists and turns ahead don't provide certainty, so some level of faith is needed.

Leaders who have open minds and are able to embrace the unknown will have a better chance of transforming their organizations. You have to be willing to rethink your organization from the ground up, centered around a new core focus. That new focus may not only put you into a different area of operations but into a completely different role, actually helping the organization become more effective, thereby bringing you new opportunities.

The first key goes back to the *Agile Manifesto* and the idea of bringing value to the customer. When that is the core principle around which everything else revolves, and when leadership is prepared to recreate the organization in that new shape (and they may not really even know what that shape looks like yet), they are in the mentality that will bolster them and their teams through their transformation.

THE CIO'S CHALLENGE

From a leadership standpoint, the CIO can have some challenges if the organization doesn't recognize the importance of the position.

According to a survey by Gartner, on average, fewer than half of CIOs report directly to the CEO, instead reporting to the CFO or another business area.[12] The further down in the org chart the CIO is, the less likely he/she will be at the table helping lead the thought that shapes the organization's decisions for years to come. Yet, paradoxically, IT plays a critical role in virtually all major areas of business. It's seen as a "cost center," yet it could be so much more.

In fact, Gartner advised CIOs to make it their ultimate goal to be co-creators with other business areas, "fostering a culture of collaboration and innovation across the enterprise."[13]

Where does IT sit within your organizational design? How does your culture view IT? Are you constantly trying to adapt to new requests and stay on top of projects and budget allocations that are already in progress? Do people see you as a go-to partner for innovation? Even better, are you an initiative-taker who leads innovation not only in your own area but also in partnership with others such as business, finance, and HR?

Your positioning as a leader depends on your ability to become this collaborative partner — a guide and mentor for the rest of the business. Your company's ability to achieve its goals also depends on its recognition of the importance of IT in the C-suite.

Gartner's data showed that only 48 percent of digital initiatives meet or exceed business outcome targets in general. However, those organizations whose CIOs have what Gartner defined as co-ownership of digital delivery from "end to end," which it identified as its "digital vanguard" companies, achieved a much higher success rate — 71 percent.[14]

If you're already in such a position, that's great. You've got one less hurdle to overcome. And if you're not, don't worry; you can get there. Either way, the next step is to understand what it takes to reach the level of transformation you'll need to become a championship-level team. The first step starts with you as a leader.

A STARTING FORMULA FOR SUCCESS

When my team and I work with leaders, we focus on two specific aspects of the leadership function: catalyst leadership and organizational agility.

Executive Level Leadership: From Standard-Bearer to Change Maker

One important point leaders (and managers) need to know is what their roles will look like in the new "future state" organization.

There's a saying about the difference between leaders and managers: Managers are working in the business, while leaders are working on the business to make it better.

That difference — what they're doing — doesn't change in this new paradigm. What changes significantly, however, is how they're doing it.

The first thing both groups need to recognize is that they must make the change first in themselves — to "be the change," as Gandhi said. That's the main way to support it throughout the whole organization. It isn't something either group can direct their subordinates on while they sit apart on the sidelines and measure performance.

Executive-level leaders — those working on making the business better —will really need to embrace and ultimately lead not only the transformation but also the need to be clear about the "why" and to be open and transparent on the approach to get there. They need to catalyze change in the organization; they need to instigate and accelerate the reaction for people getting through the change.

Executive leaders are used to waving the flag, leading the charge to conquer the next market or achieve the next corporate goal. But with a business agility focus, this role changes. They're leading a series of experiments. So, their path to the future is more a set of possible paths, with maybe none of them being "right."

Figure 5.1 The Leader's New Role

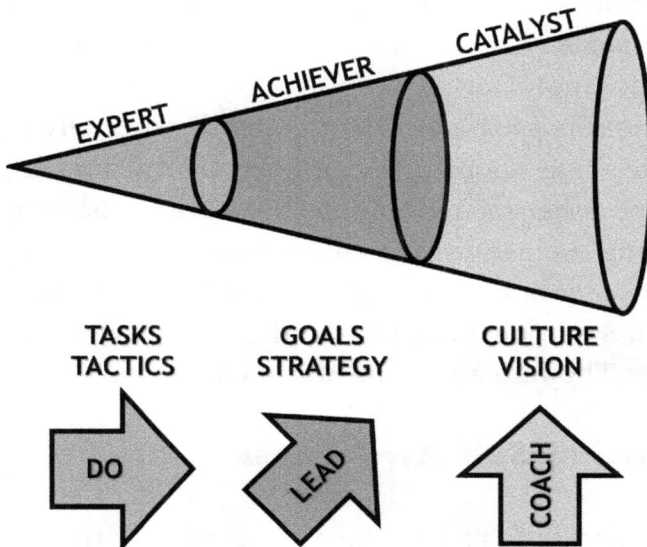

EXPERT   ACHIEVER   CATALYST

| TASKS | GOALS | CULTURE |
| TACTICS | STRATEGY | VISION |

DO   LEAD   COACH

As leaders develop, they are often recognized for their expertise and ability to "get things done" through a tactical focus on tasks. As they advance their capabilities and influence, they are asked to identify goals and strategies to achieve them and to rally people to their cause through traditional capabilities in leading followers. Today's Agile leaders, however, serve as catalysts for growth, development, and sustainable success through a focus on culture and long-term vision.

But the catalyst-minded leader goes beyond judging things as right and wrong, one and zero. Right and wrong present a limited view of possibilities. If we take the view that in a complex environment, it's hard to discern absolutes like right/wrong, we start to see it more as degrees of effectiveness.

In that case, the catalyst leader can start to make multiple simultaneous bets and turn up the dial on the ones that seem positive while dialing down the ones that aren't. This differs dramatically from the traditional approach of placing one bet at a time that either succeeds or fails, where you win or lose, or you are right or wrong. Instead, the outcome of each bet is a chance to learn and adapt — and place more bets.

Thinking in this way can be hard, especially if you're also thinking about realigning the organizational structure and other related things. You have to recognize that it's going to change over and over. Whether you find the right answer or not, the right answer isn't going to be right forever. So, leaders need to see themselves as catalysts for change. They are always agents of change.

Practicing Self-Awareness

The leaders who've been most successful at transforming their organizations are also the most effective at transforming themselves. Without that internal transformation, it's not possible to achieve the external one.

In fact, one of the most critical skills during this process is self-awareness.

Whether or not you begin with this skill — and many of our clients did not — you can learn it along the way.

It really helps the process because it can help a leader see when they're getting in their own way. Self-aware leaders tend to recognize when they are falling back into old habits or doing something that isn't aligned with the overarching goals.

In addition, when you demonstrate this skill, you set a good example for your team members to practice it, too — and that's also productive. By doing so, they will recognize and correct their own mistakes before you have to point them out. They'll be more likely to understand their own strengths and weaknesses and ask for help from others when needed.

Self-awareness doesn't have a downside, and it benefits everyone at every level.

Create a Change Leadership Team (CLT)

Many people can view "change management" as just another industry buzzword, but if you truly understand change management practices and how to use them productively, you'll start off strong. I'm including this part here because establishing this as a focus area early on can be crucial to overall long-term success.

One valuable way to use leadership in this effort is to create a Change Leadership Team (CLT) to guide the overall transformation and organizational change management (OCM) needs. This group is instilled with special responsibility to continuously sense the needs of the organization as they guide the transformation journey.

For instance, in Perry's huge data migration and new system implementation, he also faced a complex political situation. First off, other areas already questioned why they'd gone with the new system. It would do basically the same things the old one did, but just better and faster. Yet nothing that was a quantum step forward for their business. To add to their frustration, the old system still had to be maintained and paid for while setting up the new one. So, they saw this change as taking a bunch of capacity from the IT team, and the current system and all those using it getting less support.

And all of this — maintaining the old system, paying for it, and having only partial support for it — would be going on for three years (and they knew it would be more like five).

To address the situation, the company created a CLT led by Perry. Throughout the rest of the transformation, this group was responsible for providing transparency and consistent communication, tracking the overall progress of the transformation, and addressing impediments within the organizational system.

One thing Perry did immediately was to assemble a cross-functional group of key influencers and change agents and authorize them to seek out and address the systemic issues. They not only communicated outward, but they also identified and collected information, concerns, and ideas from key stakeholders from both inside and outside IT.

The CLT was not managing the project; it was leading the transformation. In this role, its members worked to make the process more transparent to the rest of the company and get feedback to make things clearer. They invited others in key areas to Sprint Reviews to engage them, allow them to see what was happening, and listen to their feedback and concerns.

One of these areas was the business side, specifically the customer support area — the primary user of the new system being implemented. Traditional IT projects oftentimes keep the business folks at arm's length, but part of the CLT's goal was to pull them in as close as possible. This approach can sometimes feel like a blessing and a curse to the business group.

The business group quickly realized that this gave them much more power to influence what was going on, which was exciting — it was what they had wanted. However, it also required more work from them than they expected. They realized they were going to need to actively and consistently participate throughout the initiative instead of the traditional approach where they shared their two cents and then waited for everything to get done a few years down the road. It wasn't going to be an occasional side thing they'd do for an hour a week. This was real collaboration, which takes time and commitment. But they actually got to make a lot of the decisions.

With these role shifts, the company not only tackled the project itself; they began to unlock and disassemble their Rube Goldberg machine and set up a much more agility-focused framework. Along with this focus, the CLT also facilitated transparency at higher levels, such as having the top-level VPs participate in monthly reviews to engage them in the process. Communication began to improve, and the group had much better engagement at all levels. This was the key to the transformation's success.

A NEW CENTER OF AUTHORITY

Business agility challenges the traditional leadership model in multiple ways. Instead of the traditional top-down, hierarchical structure in which the bulk of authority is at the top, Agile takes the authority to where it's needed most. You might think it goes to the teams solving the problems. However, in its simplest terms, if the main focus of Agile is to bring value to the customer, then ultimately, the real authority is actually in the hands of the customer. Their needs become the "boss," so to speak. Because teams work directly with the customer, they are vested with the authority to provide that value, although, obviously, limitations can apply.

The idea of giving up some authority to teams can be worrisome for leaders who are used to being the boss. As I've already mentioned, authority brings a level of comfort. Giving it up seems like self-sabotage. And yet, that's exactly what we ask our clients to do. It seems counterintuitive at first, but it eventually begins to make sense when you see the bigger picture. But before that, let's look a little more at our command-control organization to analyze how it's getting in its own way.

STAY THE COURSE AFTER THE INITIAL PROJECT

When we create an initial roadmap and establish an approach to get to that future state situation, we're not thinking in terms of months but in years. It can take three to five years of sustained effort to fully dismantle the Rube Goldberg machine and establish the new organizational system.

And it's crucial to remember this important fact: You're still not "finished." This is just the beginning of something that won't be finished.

It's important to keep this in mind, even when things get tough. Each time an organization's leadership loses focus on the transformation and moves on to a new shiny object, they lose credibility, and their team gets more skeptical.

Stay the course. It will be worth it in the long run. According to the Business Agility Institute, it can take two to three years for companies to see significant benefits in business agility, and that improvement continues as time goes on.[15]

Here's a way to think about what "staying the course" looks like from the standpoint of forming a Change Leadership Team (CLT). You've originally formed it as a specialized team with a targeted purpose, but when does the "specialness" go away? What happens when the purpose or first change initiative is "achieved"? You have three choices:

- **Option 1: Dissolve.** You could decide to just dissolve your CLT because you're "finished" transforming. However, what's really going on? Are you ever really finished transforming? Does this signal that you're just going back to the way you used to do things?

- **Option 2: Maintain.** Your CLT may live on in some form as a specialized group, guiding the organization through further transformation in other areas, projects, etc.

- **Option 3: Integrate.** Your CLT lives on and evolves and expands to encompass all your management personnel. It's no longer special or a separate group. It's now just the way managers operate within the new world. It leads change and has a defined and consistent approach to it for the long term.

Option 3 is the most successful version, but I've seen companies do Option 2 with some success as well. The worst choice is Option 1, which means the company is likely to eventually fall back into old habits and methods.

I'll say it again: No matter what you tell yourself, you're never "finished."

Ever.

THE NEW NORMAL

Thinking "never finished" can be discouraging to those who like to think in terms of projects with set end dates. I get it: Crossing off a task gives you a nice dopamine hit; finishing a major project is more like a dopamine rush.

But which is more exciting: running the same old marathon, day in and day out, or coming to work every day with an empowered team ready to find innovative ways to delight your ever-evolving customers?

I don't know about you, but I'm for the latter.

To get to that place, we have to accept that change is the new normal, and that's a good thing.

That's what business agility is all about. Change doesn't have to be frightening or out of control. It can be exciting. It can be fun. We can even lead it. And we can be equipped to handle whatever comes our way.

If you can be in that mental space, you're farther down the path to success than you might realize.

As we move into the next chapter, we'll look more at another facet of this shift from "end-goal" thinking as we stop focusing on projects and think instead in terms of products.

CHAPTER 6

PRODUCTS VS. PROJECTS

A key aspect of business agility is shifting the operational focus and management from project-centric to product-centric. This means the entire operation stops thinking in terms of managing projects and becomes focused on managing products.

The first part of that is clarifying what we mean by a "product" versus a "project" because often when we speak with clients about projects and products, they believe they are the same thing. They don't understand the difference, and they often treat projects as products.

To illustrate this, let's look at another of our clients, a financial services company, and their situation when they came to us.

When we began working with them around 2018, they had recently gone through an organizational transition. They wanted to start down the Agile path, so as we began working with them, one of the things we naturally needed to discuss was their product organization.

A fun game I play sometimes is to go to companies, knock on their door, and ask, "How many products do you have?" Inevitably, everyone in the company seems to have a different answer. With this company, we were working with a sponsor team, so we asked them to do a version of this.

We challenged them: "Go out and poll your people — just informally so it doesn't feel like an official survey. Ask them how many products they think you have, and what they are."

They talked to more than a hundred different people, and the answers they received ranged everywhere between sixteen and seventy-four.

"That's crazy!" you might think. "How can so many people in the same company have such different answers?" However, this is very typical. It happens with most of our clients.

One of the main problems is that everyone defines a product differently. Some people think, "Oh, this system we have is a product," even though it's only used internally. Some think of customer support as a product, or even phone support, website support, and email support as three different products.

There are others who realize the product is something provided for the external customer, but they think every variation for it is a different product. For instance, if a company is a toothpaste manufacturer, they may have twenty-five different variations of toothpaste. There's the bubblegum flavor, the mint flavor, the chocolate flavor; then there's the two-ounce size of the mint flavor versus the six-ounce size of the mint flavor. So, a person in that company might see each of these as a different product.

That was happening in the case of this company, too. To help them brainstorm and try to narrow things down, we held an intensive week-long workshop for ten of their strategic leaders, involving the executive team as well. As we led them through the process of uncovering the true product around which we would design the organization, we looked for ways we could group the products together. Finally, we came up with an end total they were satisfied with — three.

Yes, that's right. They went from thinking they had 16–74 products to three.

Your first question is probably, how did we get from such a big potential number to such a small one? Basically, it came down to how things could be grouped together strategically to focus on customer value.

For instance, they had a loan product, and they also managed parking payment systems, as well as toll systems. To them, each of those three things was different. Except, once we started looking at them, they were exactly the same. For each one, they sent invoices, processed payments, sent delinquency notices, and so on. The main difference was the letterhead on the invoice and the bank routing number for payment. Besides that, it was pretty much the same. That's it. It's the same system, the same data. You're still taking payments, and you're still sending the same letters, basically with a different letterhead.

So, instead of having "debt collection," "tolls," and "parking," all of those rolled together to become "payment systems." That was one of the three products. They followed the same process for the other two.

The advantage of this small number of products was that it allowed them to get really focused and think about how to make the business more efficient and aligned to deliver maximum value, both to customers and to themselves. Suddenly, they were no longer trying to manage toll payments any differently from how they were managing debt-collection payments. They were just managing the ways to process those transactions efficiently.

As you get to that higher-level thinking, operational efficiency not only gets easier, but opportunities also become much more obvious. When your product is payment systems, you suddenly start identifying more of the same customer types who could use that type of system. The clutter is out of your thinking. This is exactly what happened with our client.

THE PROBLEMS WITH PROJECT-FOCUSED OPERATIONS

One of the main hurdles to achieving business agility is a project-focused management system. Before I go further, let's go ahead and ensure we're on the same page with what I mean by a "project" versus a "product."

A project is temporary; it starts and ends. The success of a project is often defined by whether or not we delivered the full scope of work on time and on budget. When it ends, it's over, and the people and resources are redistributed, and they move on to other things.

A product is a long-lived entity that continues until we turn it off. We continue to maintain and enhance a product for the long-term benefit of its customers and stakeholders.

According to the Scrum Guide, "A product is a vehicle to deliver value. It has a clear boundary, known stakeholders, well-defined users or customers. A product could be a service, a physical product, or something more abstract."[16]

Often, projects are used to launch a product. A temporary effort is initiated to launch the initial version of a product, and then the project team disperses. The problem is that the product is now live... and we need to take care of it, maintain it, and address customer needs and feedback. It will continue to live forever, or until we turn it off.

Think about a product we all probably use called Amazon.com. It's not going to end; it just keeps going. Its owners will keep maintaining, enhancing, and innovating it until, at some point, it's obsolete, and they turn it off.

In a project-based organization, enhancements would mean starting a new project and defining the scope and budget to address these needs. In a product-based organization, teams are allocated to the product for the long term, and their job every day is to maintain, enhance, and innovate the product. No need for reallocation of people, stops and starts, or budget arguments. The company just invests in the product for the long term, and the teams work on the most important things needed to keep the product's customers happy in the short and long term.

The problem is that while a project is a goal, it isn't necessarily connected to the customer, nor is it connected to anything else. On their own, projects can exist in silos, and everyone works to complete them without really thinking about how they affect other projects, other products, the customer, or other aspects of the organization. The project manager is focused on completing the project, and they're in control of that, but they don't necessarily understand the needs of the customer.

WHY PRIORITIZING PRODUCT MANAGEMENT MAKES SENSE

A product, unlike a project, is connected to the customer — or it should be. (If you're creating products that customers aren't using, that's another issue entirely.) It centers around the customer and their needs, as well as your areas of expertise. It connects you to them and them to you.

Theoretically, the product delivery and its relevant value should form the center of focus for your operations. When you are product-driven, you are naturally more customer-centric and value-driven. It's just inherent in the perspective.

From this perspective, value delivery is never "finished." We're just continuing to listen to customer feedback to make the next round of changes and additions to achieve what they're asking for. We're focused on delivering that value versus finishing the project by the deadline.

Product-Centric Management: The Benefits

Here are several benefits of focusing on products versus projects:

- **Quicker timelines.** Projects, with their traditional waterfall approach, usually have extensive timelines. Product enhancements can be planned and handled in small increments that are easier to manage and still serve the customer.

- **Quicker response time.** Products allow the team to adjust quickly when the customer's needs change.

Because the team is organized around the product and the relevant customer feedback, they don't need to initiate a new project or submit a change request. They just do the work. They also don't have to plan around long waterfall schedules or task dependencies.

- **Less waste/Lower costs.** Think about how many waterfall projects linger on, over time and beyond budget, only for management to realize belatedly that they're totally obsolete due to some unforeseen variable or market shift. How much do these setbacks cost? Avoiding them through incremental problem-solving can save a company millions.

- **More transparency.** Products, at least those managed in an Agile way, provide constant transparency to stakeholders in order to seek feedback and adjust priorities.

- **Happier teams.** When teams see a direct, value-focused end result to their efforts — when they see how what they're doing is actually making a difference — it is a huge morale boost. Contrast that to a team that's focused on completing a project on time and under budget but doesn't see the purpose of the project — and whose members might also be doing several other similar projects. They're pulled in several directions, and they don't see how they're contributing value in any of them. Their morale will probably not be as high as the dedicated, product-driven team.

In fact, according to Gartner's data, "In the next five years, CIOs expect around 70 percent of work to be done using a product-centric model."[17] The benefits can't be ignored. And most important, a product-centered focus doesn't just apply to software development — it works with any type of business and any product.

If It Works, Why Aren't We Doing It More?

Again, we can look at traditional management reasoning and practices to understand why we're not coming from the product-oriented focus more often. It actually just makes sense that this is where we are right now. It's a natural stage in the evolution.

In traditional management, control, measurement, and efficiency dominate thinking. Focusing on projects makes perfect sense in that they lend the air of predictability we crave. They can be measured. I can say, "We're 68 percent done with this project," and everyone feels like they know what's going on. We can forecast and plan for budgets, track time, and determine end dates. We have a schedule. We feel like we know what's going to happen, at least in theory.

However, as I've noted previously, all of these are actually moving targets. The words "68 percent done" don't necessarily mean it's going to take another 32 percent of the time already spent to get the project done. The market conditions, unforeseen obstacles, and other variables — even conflicts with other projects — can easily throw the schedule off track. We don't really know what's going to happen — we just pretend we do. It goes back to that comfort zone of feeling like we're in control.

Meanwhile, as we're focused on controlling, predicting, and reacting to all these variables, the reality is that the customer has changed his mind four times and now needs something totally different. Because our focus is on the project, not the customer, we are not aware of their changing needs and continue working on things that are no longer relevant.

And because we're used to thinking from a project-related focus, we don't totally understand the situation. We're working and thinking in silos that don't allow us to see any other way to work. Getting out of that mindset can be tough, especially when your success as a leader is measured by your projects and not by customer value delivery. Only by looking at it from a broader perspective and shifting our focus from a blinders-on, top-down control mindset can we get out of the project-focused fragmentation. That's why senior-level leadership's active involvement in leading the transition is so crucial — without that, there's not enough authority to shift focus where needed.

DESIGNING AND MANAGING THE PRODUCT PORTFOLIO

You naturally want to know how all of this will look when it's set up, and you're probably already asking questions about how all of this could work in your organization.

First, let's take a look at the major areas we need to assess to make sure your product portfolio makes sense and is managed correctly.

Strategic Alignment

The goal with strategic product alignment is to align the strategy to the execution. In other words, every aspect of the organization needs to reflect the product strategy, from organizational design itself to the policies and processes governing the execution, including how the company is investing in innovation and delivery. This is what C-level leaders should be focused on. Strategic alignment is what shifts the focus from a project-oriented approach to a product-oriented one.

The first thing to look at is your current product portfolio and how you're prioritizing your investments into each individual product within the whole.

I often use Microsoft as an example. Let's say they have four main products: Office 365, Windows, Xbox, and the Azure Cloud. Those products are distinct. So, if we're their C-level team looking at that collection as a portfolio, we're thinking about how much to invest in each of those, and how to measure success around each.

This leads to the ideas of portfolio management, product organization, and strategic innovation, all of which come together to bring value to the customer. We have to manage the portfolio by deciding which products to keep or discontinue. We may prioritize growing one product over others. We also might have to look at whether an innovative new idea fits within an existing product or whether we should spin up a new product instead. For instance, when Microsoft decided to offer AI, they put it inside their Office 365 product rather than making it a product on its own.

Strategic innovation is about enhancing your portfolio through intentional innovation. Some companies that prioritize innovation don't set any rules around it. They say something like, "All right, we're giving you 20 percent of your time to spend just letting random things come into your head and following up on them." That may work sometimes, but it's not strategic. Instead, we help clients create an intentional, structured approach to innovation that establishes a pipeline validating customer needs, product/market fit, and financial viability. The approach is to continually test ideas through future-looking criteria and pivot early and often to navigate potential options and find the ideas that show potential and increasingly positive results.

Most of the time, you'll be innovating in a space you already understand. But not always. There are some types of innovation that aren't as logical — but they still work. So, there aren't a lot of restrictions in our process; the main aspect is that it happens in a structured framework to deliver a pipeline of viable ideas to enhance the portfolio from a potential customer value standpoint.

The other factor in strategic alignment is the organizational structure. How do we align our organization to support the products? When we add a new product, have we also planned for the organizational elements to support it? If we're adding functionality, do we need to add more support areas to handle that? Organizational design considerations are not static, but continually evolving based on external factors as well as the emerging innovation capabilities of the organization.

Product Management

Once you have products, they need to be managed at the product level, individually. Each is basically run as a distinct business unit. The activities we focus on in this segment are product ownership, product strategy, and customer focus. This entire focus is to maximize the value delivered by teams working on each product.

Each product needs its own product manager/owner with a distinct set of priorities. This is the reason why it's important to narrow down the number of products to as small a number as possible to ensure that, as an organization, we are working on the highest priorities possible. If we look back at our financial services client, imagine if they really had seventy-four products. For each of those, they'd need a product manager and at least one dedicated team. It also means those seventy-four different products each would have a number one priority. And I guarantee those seventy-four different number-one priorities are not all equal, and they shouldn't be treated as such. That would have been a nightmare for them to try to manage, which is why consolidating and reducing the number of products in the organization is crucial. It provides clarity, transparency, and focus to ensure we're maximizing the value delivered for each one.

Product ownership revolves around the internal and external aspects of managing the product. For instance, who are the internal stakeholders? How can the operations be transparent to those groups? How can we engage with the teams, prioritize important enhancements, and make tradeoff decisions?

And obviously, we're looking at the customer. What's their persona? How can we bring them more value? How can we get feedback from them? Product strategy is related to how we market to the customer, and all those activities. We also use specific tools to help clients with those things. This gets more into the tactical side, and it is very specific to each client and their customer base.

Where Projects Fit

Projects don't necessarily go away in this framework. However, wherever possible, they should be associated with a product and how it provides, enhances, or supports customer value in some way. If not, we might want to re-think if that project should exist.

For instance, we recently worked with a client in the banking industry to align their list of projects to their newly defined set of products. Sometimes, it's hard to break out of the temporary start-stop-reallocate mentality of projects, but the key is to connect the dots on which product area seems like the best fit. But there are cases where it just may not make direct sense.

For example, let's say you have a project to migrate to a new data center. That probably doesn't make sense to roll up under any one product alone. But if all your people are on product-related teams, the work of that project might become part of each product area's backlog in order to support the migration based on overall organizational priorities. Then, it becomes a conversation across all those product managers to determine the priority of that migration versus customer-facing priorities. And they need to consider that the data migration does enhance the customer experience (in terms of things like security, scalability, reliability, etc.), so it is a situation they can still connect back to customer value; it's just a few extra layers to connect the dots and prioritize with a strategic understanding of long-term value.

There — now we've connected the dots. Everything comes back to how we serve the customer, and all the activities of serving the customer tie back to a product.

Figuring out which individual product you want to tie something like the network infrastructure to can be more complex, especially when it supports most or all of your products and is used by everyone in the organization, whether they're in a product area or in a back-office support role. Often, a client will just put something like network infrastructure in the product that is most needed, though the network serves all their products. That way, the infrastructure updates are prioritized with that high-priority product.

In addition, as new projects come up, we look at whether we allocate them to the existing product areas, or whether we need to spin up a new product. Sometimes, that's where innovation takes us. If something doesn't fit under any of our current products, then the executive leadership needs to look at whether or not to invest in spinning up a new product — not just the product itself, but the team and other support elements to continue it.

SHIFTING TO PRODUCT-CENTERED OPERATIONS

Making the shift in your organization first requires a shift in thinking — and sometimes, that's the hardest part.

Start with the Customer

When we go into a client's environment, we do a lot of this, as it's often difficult for a client to assess the situation objectively. When the client is embedded in something day in and day out, and their comfort zone is the current status quo, it's hard to see it differently — we all have this challenge with the things in our daily environment. Remember: For our financial services client, it took a week-long workshop with facilitators to come to the final determination. And before that there were about two months of workshop preparation and data collection. So don't get discouraged if you can't do it in a day.

The first thing to identify is the set of customers you're already dealing with, and what they currently think your products are. You don't necessarily take this as the final answer, but it's a very informative step, especially when you dig into those customers and start seeing commonalities among them.

Remember the financial client who had three different "products" that combined into one called "payment systems"? When we first looked at the customer for tolls, loans, and parking, we had three different personas. But as we dug deeper, we found they were very closely related and had the same kinds of needs, with a few minor differences.

Once you dig deeper into the customer personas and have a first pass at some potential products, then start asking some questions to frame up ways you might further consolidate or validate the potential products. Here are some things to ask yourselves while categorizing your current product list:

- Do any of these use the same type of data? For instance, customer attributes (name, address, demographics), financial information, or transaction reporting?

- Do they use the same technology or systems? Examples include having the same website, applications, or customer data management system.

- Do you deliver them in a similar way? Do they go through the same or similar channels like a website, retail store shelves, or a mobile application?

- Do you service them in a similar way? For example, do you use the same customer service phone number and personnel, the same help website, or the same third-party support group to handle customer problems?

- Do they have the same customer types? For instance, if the customer goes to a bank, they can get a savings account, a checking account, a CD, or whatever, but it's still all the same type of person getting that stuff. So, are checking, savings, and CDs different high-level products, or could the product just be "banking for consumers"?

- Do you follow roughly the same processes for them? Remember our financial services client who was sending out the same kind of letters, just on different letterheads?

Try to identify the product in as broad a category as possible, and from the standpoint of the customer. Is the product bubblegum toothpaste, or just toothpaste with multiple varieties? Or is it really toothpaste at all? What if it's actually "mouth care," with toothpaste as one feature, along with mouthwash and floss? Those kinds of answers are nuanced based on the complexities of the situation, but they are worth evaluating if you really want to provide transparency and maximize value.

Create Your New Structure

When you have your product portfolio established, you'll want to restructure your operations from a project-centric to a product-centric focus. This requires setting up your teams. It's a good idea to determine your product managers first so they can start to conceptualize the details of the product and their vision for the future. This will help to determine what's needed now and in the near future in terms of the skills and capabilities of the teams that will be formed to support and deliver the product.

This process can take more time than you might predict, and you need to think carefully about the skill sets of the potential product managers. This group is crucial for success. They need authority from the organization to make decisions, and they need to feel comfortable doing so. They also need to be available to collaborate with the team and with customers/stakeholders. It's a full-time job, not a side gig. They should also be knowledgeable about the product, the market, and customer needs. Equally important, they need to be passionate about the product and the value it provides.

You may actually already have people in your organization who would be a fit, but you may not. You might have people who are trainable to shift to that role, or you might need to hire new staff. Those are big questions you'll need to consider. If you get the right people into the product manager role, you'll definitely be better off as you set up your teams.

For instance, it's usually good practice to shift folks from the business team to product management, especially because they're usually more aligned around customer needs, which is a key component of product management. In fact, it's probably one of the most important skill sets.

Be wary of just "blanket shifting" roles or making sweeping changes across the board. For instance, one of our clients decided to just turn all their project managers into product managers. However, they didn't consider that while there are some overlapping skill sets, product management has a much different focus than project management. Project managers think in terms of deadlines and schedules and often internal stakeholders, but they don't necessarily understand the external customer and market shifts. They might not feel comfortable making decisions about things they aren't knowledgeable about.

A product manager is really more at the VP level, with serious business impact on their shoulders, but a project manager is often at a lower level and may not fully appreciate, or have experience dealing with, that type of responsibility — and they may not be comfortable with it. It's not that it won't necessarily work, but they probably need more training, coaching, and mentoring to be successful in the role.

We'll look more at how this will work in the "Organizing True Teams" chapter. But for now, just keep in mind that having the right people in place is crucial for success. If you understand your products and what knowledge your teams will need to best serve the customer, it will be easier to identify the skills, knowledge, and experience your product managers will need.

Create a Roadmap for Change

Obviously, you're not going to just start shifting everything to the new portfolio on Day One. However, you can now include it as part of your future-state roadmap and how you'll approach that shift over time.

After you've considered your current situation and defined your future-state products, you'll be able to create your roadmap showing how to get there.

Remember: You're building for the long term. The products will support that vision for the long-term future. To ensure you're creating a viable organizational design, consider everything that goes into making that product successful. In addition to building the product, you'll need to ensure you address considerations such as product delivery, marketing, customer support, customer feedback loops, and other ongoing needs. Since you'll be realigning your current functional structure into a product-oriented structure, you'll need to think of each of these elements specific to each product. Oftentimes, planners overlook this. They're thinking about how to build and maintain the product, but not all the other support elements around it.

Once you define those areas, you can start identifying the skills you need and forming your new teams.

CHAPTER 7

ORGANIZING TRUE TEAMS

Once your leadership mindset is on the right track and you have a goal for strategically aligning your organizational design and your product portfolio, as well as the other aspects of your organizational change approach, you can start taking a more detailed look at setting up your teams to deliver value while also maintaining organizational agility.

THE RIGHT TIMING TO LOOK AT TEAMS

I want to take a moment here to mention an important point: The sequence in which you work to address your leadership, products, and teams matters.

Often, when leaders come to us to help them solve their business issues, they are focused on issues they've identified with their teams — for instance, leadership feels the teams aren't performing well or need more motivation or better processes. Even if these things are true, the root issue is almost never about the teams themselves. It's almost always about the underlying organizational design, culture, and/or leadership.

In fact, that's why I've structured these three topics based on our AgileOS® principles in the order of Leaders, Products, and Teams. It is ideal to work on the Leaders segment first, setting up your leadership with the right focus and mindset. Then you'll turn to Products, mapping your future/vision and what your product portfolio will look like. Then, only after you have a clear handle on these two facets, can you successfully start your focus on the Teams segment, during which you create (or recreate) your various teams and decide on their methods and logistics. Working on the Teams segment without dealing with those other issues first is just trying to fix the symptoms instead of getting to the root cause. Without solving those other issues, whatever you do to improve team performance may be beneficial in the short term but will likely only be short-lived.

To create high-performing teams, you need to first focus on ensuring they are real teams. Doing this often requires resetting the definition of "team" in your organization, clearly defining its focus, and creating the organizational environment that will promote high performance.

FIRST THINGS FIRST: REDEFINING TEAMS

In a traditional management structure, managers talk about teams, but they aren't real teams, as far as I'm concerned.

Usually, when managers refer to "their team," they are referring to the people who simply report to the same manager and are likely in the same functional area doing the same type of work. An example would be a QA manager who describes the group of eight QA testers as the "QA team."

Another misuse of the team concept is when people refer to a "project team" consisting of people whose time is temporarily and partially allocated toward completing sets of tasks on a larger project, alongside other temporarily partially allocated people.

In both cases, these are not teams in the way we need to define teams in the context of creating high-performing Agile teams.

A team is a group of people committed to a common goal where each member is dedicated to one, and only one, team. High-performing Agile teams are autonomous, self-managing teams that have all the skills and authority to deliver end-to-end value to their customers. Going back to the basketball team analogy: We want a cross-functional set of people who are dedicated to the common goal of winning the championship together, and they will do what's needed, have each other's backs, and be selfless and resilient in the face of adversity in order to win.

With that in mind, the "QA team" example falls apart in that they cannot deliver value to the customer if their only skillset is testing, as they are missing many of the capabilities needed to deliver value by themselves. In the basketball analogy, this would be a group of point guards who can pass, but we're missing team members who can shoot, defend, and rebound.

In the project team example, the group members are not dedicated to a single team or a common goal. They are typically assigned to many different projects, each having its own goal. And the person's goal is simply to complete their tasks efficiently. While this might be a valid way to accomplish tasks given a limited set of skilled people, it's simply not a team. In the basketball team analogy, this group may have all the skills temporarily, but after the point guard brings the ball up during the first quarter, they may leave the court to go across the street and play in a different game.

In both cases, a more accurate term for these collections of people might be a "work group." Certainly not anywhere near what I would describe as a team. Would you?

If I were asked to play the same role — say, point guard — on four different teams, some of which might be playing each other at some point, what real ownership would I have for the teams' results? I'd see myself more as an individual contributor than as a part of a group, and sometimes, I'd have to decide which team I am playing on if two of my teams are playing each other.

How can those teams play their best if they aren't practicing and working together exclusively? Each team has a culture and a style they develop organically based on the individual skill sets and the goals. Trying to juggle different goals, interactions, and processes would create a lot of challenges for the players in this scenario.

And that's basketball, where the goals are clear: getting the ball to someone who can score and keeping the other team from doing so. But in business, there are more complicated scenarios at play.

To work on a project, functional team members don't have the autonomy to make most decisions. Instead, they have to work through a supervisor to get permission to do whatever they need to do. Sometimes, it's not clear which supervisor has the ownership or authority for that particular decision. If there is conflict between a software engineer, a tester, and a business analyst, which of the three managers wins? (Well, if you've been in IT, you know which one wins, but you see the point, right?)

Also, projects may need certain skills for part of the project, so the project team might pull in another functional area or department where needed, but only for the short term. That other functional area might be working on ten other projects, so they aren't necessarily prioritizing any of them in relation to customer value. They may just be putting out the fires that smoke the most, or doing the easier stuff because it's quick, regardless of how important it is.

Setting Up a Solid Team Structure

When I refer to a team, what I mean is a dedicated, cross-functional team focused on achieving a single goal and working together to make it happen. The approach is dynamic, not fragmented, and everyone is all-in to achieve the goal. They are not allocated to multiple teams or focused on differing goals at once.

This is what a basketball team does. It has one goal: to win. Its players all perform their functions with that goal in mind. They don't play for other teams, and they aren't juggling different priorities. Some of the time, many of them are sitting on the bench, but when it's their turn to play, they're expected to show up ready to do their part to achieve the goal.

In an Agile business, the team structure revolves around a particular product, and its sole function is to deliver value to the customer. Therefore, the team structure needs to include every facet needed to deliver value. This means your teams have to be cross-functional. You want the people on the team to have all the skills, information, and authority needed to get the work done, regardless of what function they perform.

For instance, one company we worked with was in a highly regulated industry. They were designing software, but they also had legal implications to consider when making design decisions. So, for probably six to nine months, instead of calling on someone outside the team from the legal department all the time and waiting on those decisions, the company embedded an attorney on the software team to make the decisions fast and keep going. That was a much different way of thinking. They previously focused on using the lawyers' time efficiently — but now they were focused on the value-delivery aspect and getting the work done effectively by eliminating delays.

The teams need all the skills required to achieve the goal of delivering value to the customer via the product — even if it's just a short-term situation to solve specific problems. What we can learn from the previous example is that if you're delivering products in a highly regulated environment, involve your legal group in the team's structure.

The structure will, in part, depend on what you're producing. However, your previous planning should inform the types of skill sets you need. If you look at the required skill sets first and then start looking at how you can combine them to create your team, you'll realize that some people may currently have more than one of these skill sets, possibly already in the combination you need, and they could perform more than one type of task on the team. If not, focus on training people who are willing to learn and build new skills over time, ideally through collaboration with others on the team who have that skill.

Teams vs. Individual Heroes

One of the problems that the teams in the fragmented, project-focused structure face is that they often view their contributions from an individual standpoint. They're not embedded into any team. Their incentives can even reinforce this mindset by rewarding them for how many times they were able to do a particular type of task or how few errors they made, despite the fact that there's no clear way to measure whether those things brought any value to the customer.

When leaders talk about teamwork, but their rewards focus on individual performance, this creates a disconnect. But again, the problem is organizational — it's not even the leader's fault. It's just a symptom of the bigger issue. The structural issues need to be solved first so the team can flourish as a true team.

This means that, with a business agility focus, team culture needs to shift just as leadership culture did. It's similar, too — just as leadership culture shifts from a "hero" to "catalyst" mode, team culture will be shifting from an "individual hero" to a "high-performing team" perspective. In this mindset, the team wins together. There isn't a single star who is always noticed for saving the day. The whole team is the star that continually delivers value and delights the customer. The whole team is responsible for the success or failure of achieving the goal, which is delighting the customer.

Agile Mastery

Agile mastery is also crucial for business agility. You can have a true cross-functional team, but if they aren't also trained in Agile methods, they won't be able to deliver in that respect. For instance, do you have a Scrum master who really understands how to support the team and build their skills? One of the mistaken assumptions is that the Scrum master is just a facilitator. But they're not — they're actually more like a tough-love parent or coach. They challenge the team to be the best it can be. They call BS and look for ways the team can improve through collaboration and learning, and they help the team truly own their own destiny.

The final aspect is another degree of mastery, which we describe as multi-team collaboration or being a "team of teams." This concept is framed around the individual teams also working together to accomplish a bigger goal. They will operate within their small team but also within the larger unit. There's a great book by General Stanley McChrystal called *Team of Teams*, in which he talks about this concept in relation to military units. They are small units, but they're part of a larger organization trying to accomplish a bigger goal. They're self-organizing but within the context of the other teams with which they are collaborating.[18] This is the same concept.

We use different techniques to help teams not just have their own individual team identity but also pair up in the larger units to achieve bigger goals more effectively. When we explain this idea, we often say that in this scenario, one plus one doesn't equal two; it's actually like one plus one equals three. Because the power of multiple teams working together can multiply the potential outcomes for customers instead of just adding to it.

CREATE THE RIGHT TEAM ENVIRONMENT

When you're redesigning for business agility, it's crucial to put teams in the best environment for success. I'm not just talking about their physical space — though that is important. I'm talking about the parameters they're operating within. What are they being measured on? How are they being managed? What is their focus? Do they have the tools and information they need to make decisions and follow through?

This is why the environment starts with Agile managers.

Agile Managers vs. Traditional Managers

Managers have a different way of becoming catalysts within the new structure. I like to illustrate this with a story of a client, where one of the key managers was someone we now affectionately call "New Bob."

In the corporate world, there are managers who do all the work, managers who lead the work, and managers who coach others to do the work (see Fig. 7.1).

Figure 7.1

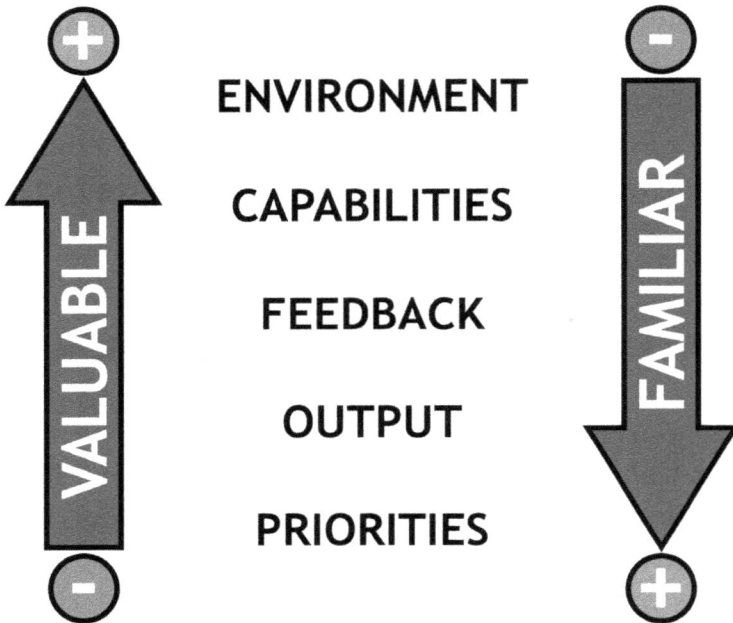

Traditional managers are most familiar with the tactical aspects of prioritizing work for their people and ensuring they follow the process and procedure toward a quality output. Agile managers allow the teams to manage these aspects themselves, while the manager focuses on higher-value aspects, such as building capabilities and solving organizational impediments and environmental roadblocks.

"Old Bob" was in the first mindset. He was a traditional manager who believed he had to do all the work and make all the decisions. He was constantly running around trying to stay on top of what was going on, and he always seemed frazzled, stressed, and overwhelmed.

He was a good guy, and he was trying to do the right thing. One of his responsibilities was to manage the IT support department, and he took a personal interest in making sure everything was getting solved. They had an automated routing system, but instead of letting it route the tickets, he had set things up to come to him so he could personally make sure everything was getting handled by the right person. To the degree that even at night, on the third shift, while he was supposed to be sleeping, if a ticket came in, he received a notification and popped out of bed to have a look. I'm not sure he had taken a vacation in five years. How could he?

Bob felt he was such a critical cog in the machine that he didn't know what would happen if he took himself out of the middle of everything. And he also felt he didn't have the time to figure out how to do that either. Plus, the company had already tried an Agile adoption previously, but due to the way they implemented it, it hadn't succeeded. So, I think he was skeptical about whether this one would get anywhere, either.

But if anyone could benefit from shifting his role, it was Bob. He meant well, but he was in the middle of everything. He could never take a day off. He was a bottleneck, and he realized it, but he didn't know how it could be any other way. He had so much pressure on him all the time, and it was taking its toll.

As part of the early phase of the Agile transformation, we started working with Bob and his team. As the team began to mature and take more ownership and responsibility, Bob started to see some light in the tunnel. He got out of the middle and started giving more authority to his team. His confidence built a little at a time. He became more comfortable and trusted that people could make good decisions on routing tickets and handling the work. He was still nervous when new people were hired, but he had his team train them and tried to stay out of that, too.

Eventually, instead of being the one making all the decisions, he was in more of a coaching and support role, helping his team succeed. He was just managing people, not in the middle of the process or doing the work. Taking a step back as he had, he could start looking at the metrics and outliers and see the patterns — certain repeat issues that seemed to pop up every one out of ten times, or maybe a ticket that sat there for more than forty-eight hours. Then he could work on those, instead of every single problem.

Everyone was surprised at this change and its results — most of all, Bob. Almost every time we saw him, he told us how much happier he was. "I don't have to make all the decisions! My team is happier, I'm happier... this is great!"

"Yeah!" we joked with him. "This is New Bob! New Bob is way happier than Old Bob." We all laughed. The joke stuck, and now we affectionately refer to him as New Bob.

Our goal is to get more managers to this end state. Managers who focus more on coaching others and letting them make their own decisions are not only more effective, they're also much happier — and so is everyone who works with them. (I'm pretty sure New Bob's staff and colleagues would agree with me on this one.)

Often, things can start out with managers like Old Bob. They're in the middle of everything, and they're in the way. Their intentions are good, but they just aren't letting the work flow.

The goal is to take a step back.

With a traditional manager, managing the work and managing the people are tightly coupled. What the Agile manager has to learn to do is pull these two things apart and then focus on managing the people while letting them manage their own work. The manager's job is to create the environment and manage the people. They do the professional development, conflict management — all the HR stuff — but don't manage the work itself. This is what New Bob learned to do very effectively.

Achieving Operational Excellence

When they're able to stand back and watch the team, managers are more able to focus on operational excellence. In other words, they start managing the system itself, not the work details.

At a training session I attended years ago, I heard a great story about a manufacturing plant that had a funny orientation process for new management hires. On the production floor, there was a circle painted on the ground, somewhat out of the way for safety purposes. The new manager was told by their supervisor, "OK, now go stand in this circle and just watch and observe. Make some mental notes about what you see. I'll be back to check on you in a little while."

After a few hours, the supervisor came back and said, "How's it going?"

"Great," the new hire replied. "Everything is running smoothly."

"OK. Keep watching, and I'll be back in a while." And the supervisor left again for another couple of hours.

This time, when they came back and asked how things were going, the new hire said, "Oh, it's good, but there seem to be some problems. I noticed a few people have to run back and forth several times for some reason. And over here, when this forklift came around the corner, he almost hit this guy."

The supervisor listened, nodded, and then left again for another couple of hours. By the end of the day, when they returned, the new hire had become horrified. "I don't know how everyone here isn't dead," they said. "And everything is so inefficient. How are we possibly still in business?"

Nothing in the plant had changed from the beginning of the day to the end. What happened was that the new hire stood back and paid close attention the entire time. The longer they observed, the more they noticed the things that were really going on instead of just glossing over them or assuming a repetitive problem was just a one-time occurrence.

This is what managers need to do instead of getting neck-deep into the work of their teams. Once you step back and start really looking at the system — at the details — you start seeing the real issues and patterns. Now, you can focus on optimizing the system by looking at the bigger picture.

Team Subculture and Environment

Part of creating an effective system is letting the team create its own subculture and identity. This can be whatever they want, and it should be fun. At one of our banking clients, one of the first teams I coached decided their team's name would be "The Farm." I think one of the teammates was well known to live on a farm, brought in fresh eggs once in a while, and always had a good story about something that happened while feeding the animals before work.

So, the team adopted this theme as their shared identity. With that theme, everything in their workspace began to take on that identity. They stopped short of bringing in hay bales, but almost everything they referenced was farm-related. They affectionately called their shared breakout room, which was the only place where you could have a private conversation, "the barn." So they'd say, "Let's go back to the barn and talk." When describing the size of the work during their planning sessions, they created a scale in farm terms. Tiny was a "baby chick," small was a "rooster," then "pig," "cow," "tractor," and so on. It made things a lot more fun and really showed off their character and identity.

Managers should support this kind of identity for teams. It helps them gel and become a more close-knit and collaborative team.

The manager should also make sure the physical environment supports teamwork. Executing on that can be harder than it sounds. We often help clients with this.

For instance, some assume they need a totally open office environment to facilitate teamwork. However, that's not actually the optimal approach. One large bank learned this the hard way when they redesigned one of their buildings to remove all the interior walls — a truly open concept like a newsroom floor.

The problem was that when the team needed to have a focused meeting, they had to find a conference room away from their actual workspace in order to have loud debate and conversation.

What you need is not a totally open office but rather an environment that lets the team communicate with one another without disturbing or being disturbed by people from other teams. If you hear everything going on in the office, it's distracting and reduces productivity. You just need to know what's going on with your team, not everyone else's.

It's, therefore, more optimal to design a team room with walls, which also provides the opportunity for the team to physically display information on the wall to make important items visible and easy to reference. An arrangement in which each team has its own room facilitates teamwork much better than an open office does.

Effectiveness vs. Efficiency

One other thing about managing teams in this new framework: Managers need to shift to a value-delivery mindset versus thinking they have to keep people busy all the time.

There's an analogy that's sometimes used in Agile books about a relay race. Say you have a 4x100 relay, which my daughter runs. If you think about it, that's very inefficient because, at any given time, three people are just standing there. But, because each of them can sprint as fast as they can for 100 meters and hand off to the next person, it's the fastest way possible to get the baton around the track. If you just have one person trying to run all 400 meters by themselves, they're tremendously slower than four people, each running 100 yards as fast as they can. For reference, the world record for men's 400m is 43.03 seconds.[19] The record for 4x100 is 36.84, which is about 15 percent faster in getting around the track.[20]

The goal of the relay race is not to keep everyone busy. It's to get the baton around the track as fast as possible. And that's sort of a rethinking about what's valuable and important within an organization. With that kind of approach, it's OK to put people from the business area, such as attorneys, on the Scrum teams because even though they may be idle some of the time, the team can have ready access when needed and get the baton around the track faster. It's not about keeping people busy all the time with what they know how to do best. It's about getting the baton around the track as fast as possible — getting the work done and getting value to the customer as fast as possible. The focus becomes less about efficiency and more about effectiveness. There's a huge difference.

Continuous Delivery

This is mainly a software aspect, so it may not relate to every team. But it goes back to the roots of Agile. Rather than developing something that has to go through different environments for development, testing, production, and so on, the team is set up so that all these things take seconds, not weeks. The team is continuously delivering what they build.

They're making small tweaks over short time periods — usually two-week Sprints — instead of giant changes that take months or even years. The team members are able to complete work and release it to production as soon as they finish it, often multiple times per day.

However, the idea applies to general team operations in any industry: the whole process is streamlined so we can deliver ongoing value improvements instead of the customer waiting weeks, months, or years for them.

TWO SUCCESSFUL TEAM TRANSFORMATIONS

Teams that go through a business agility transformation often run into interesting challenges when the rest of the company hasn't gone through the transformation yet. Let's look at how two teams handled such challenges in very different situations.

The first was a group I worked with a while ago as a consultant. I walked in the first day and started looking around at how they were working. They were following Agile practices in some ways: They had an open, team-centered workspace, and they were having Scrum meetings and doing Sprints. They all got along and seemed to feel they were a team, but they didn't appear to be getting much done — nothing seemed to be going into production.

The team did some self-reflection and realized things were getting hung up for reasons that all stemmed from one main problem: they superficially understood the process, but not the "why" underneath. First off, they weren't really working as a Scrum team. They'd come together for Sprint Planning, and then the Scrum master would say, "OK, here's all the work we're going to do." Then they'd split it up, and each person would take a chunk and go off to their cubicles to do it by themselves.

That misses the point of Scrum. The team was trying to get everything done at once by each person working on their thing by themselves. As a result, they may only get a few random things done by the end of the Sprint — and it's not necessarily the highest priority items. If they prioritize everything and then they all work together on the same top priority item until it's done, before moving on to the next, they know the priority work is getting done, and they'll have much more value to show at the end of the Sprint.

The next problem, and this was a huge reason why they were getting stalled so much, was that they weren't including final approvals in the Sprints. They'd get to the end, and everything would sort of go into a weird oblivion waiting for approval by other areas, which could take weeks or even months sometimes. So, they never knew when they would be getting something into production. They were in a heavily regulated industry, so they thought this was just how it was. This is common. Some of the biggest hurdles teams face are the things that seem to happen outside their control, with the bureaucracy and approval policies.

This problem was mainly due to a misunderstanding of the purpose behind the Sprint Review. The whole goal is to invite the stakeholders and the customer to the Sprint Review. It's not for *us*. We already know what we did — we don't need to tell ourselves again because we were there. What we need to do is show the stakeholders and the customer real, live working features and discuss their feedback collaboratively. That's the point. We show what we did, how it's real, how it works, and how to use it right now. Then we talk about what would make that even better and more valuable in the next Sprint.

Their Sprints also didn't include all the steps for delivery. Approvals were floating around out there. They didn't know when approvals would come back or how they'd address the work when they did. They were completely divorced from the rest of the company. It's funny because even the bricks-and-mortar situation showed the problem

— the functional IT group was all in the same building, but the rest of the company was in a different building.

The final problem was that even after approval, they still had to go through testing, which was a totally different environment. The reality was that they were calling twenty steps from done "almost done."

Figure 7.2.a A Common Sprint Mistake

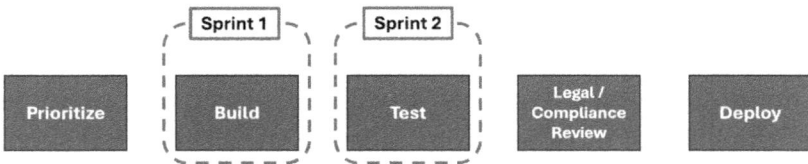

A misunderstanding of Agile delivery is to break waterfall stages out into separate sprints. For example, building a feature in Sprint 1, and testing it in Sprint 2.

Figure 7.2.b Proper Sprint Design

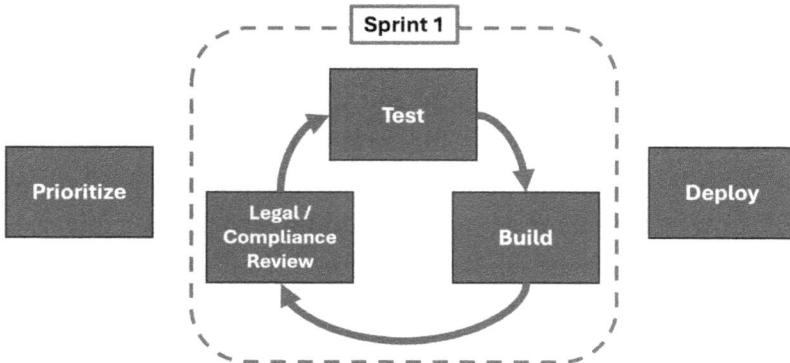

Proper Agile delivery occurs all together in a single sprint. Note that the review (validation of what is required) phase happens before testing (determining how to test the end result), which itself happens prior to building the feature. The result is more likely to meet expectations and pass the review. It's like taking an exam when you already have the answer key — it's hard to get it wrong!

The key to unlocking this problem was for the Scrum masters to realize they were empowered to solve it. They needed to take charge of delivering the value. They needed to pull in their own leadership to talk to the other C-suite folks and get things moving. When the Scrum masters understood their authority and their CIO realized they needed to be the catalyst with other senior leadership, the light bulbs came on.

So, they started including all the key personnel — legal, product management, business, etc. — in their Sprint Reviews for approvals. This resulted in a ten-minute approval process, and they were done. They also included their testing in the Sprints instead of waiting till the end or after the Sprint. They were finally using their Sprints the way they were supposed to, and they finally started getting work done in true Scrum fashion. Their entire process of delivery eventually went from taking months down to a single two-week Sprint nearly every time.

Another team that had a similar issue in a somewhat different context was in a large pharmaceutical company. They were a sub-group developing an app to streamline their clinical testing decision-making.

They started out within the main corporate environment, but because of their need to focus, corporate agreed to split them out as a separate pseudo-autonomous organization. They had their own cross-functional team, and they were in their own building across town, far away from the buttoned-down corporate HQ.

They thought of themselves as a startup company, and in many ways, they were. But while they felt like they had more leeway to try new things outside the traditional, risk-averse corporate culture, each of the individuals still carried a lot of internal corporate baggage. They'd been in corporate for twenty to thirty years, and they weren't sure how to operate as a startup.

It's tough when you're used to rigid corporate culture, and you have to break your mindset out of it. You just want to keep obeying the "authority" even though you don't have to report to them much anymore.

So on the one hand, they had succeeded in relieving themselves of too much structure, but on the other, they needed a different framework that would support their goals.

The problems here were similar to the first situation — they'd adopted Agile, but only at a surface level, and they didn't totally understand the reasons for everything. They were positive, smart, and excited. They just needed to channel that enthusiasm, intelligence, and energy into productivity. And they knew there was a lot they didn't know, so they were open-minded.

With them, the biggest light bulb went on when we were looking at how to break out their goals into daily work. They had sort of project-managed everything in milestones, and they were like the other team I mentioned — people were all individually working on things all at once. Not as a team. Like five basketball players all on the court at once, playing another team, but each playing one-on-one. It doesn't make sense.

So, when they shifted to working as a true team, they started realizing how much they learned with each new piece of work they finished, and they could reprioritize with feedback and focus on the next most important piece. Suddenly, their milestones were happily obsolete. At the eighteen-month mark, they had delivered more working value than they had planned to do in the first three years. And then they got authorized to just keep going.

PILOT TEAMS: MANAGING CHANGE INCREMENTALLY

As I've mentioned, all of this doesn't happen at once. It's a process. Often, companies begin with one team focused on a particular product/project and then expand that success through others. These "pilot teams" allow us to test a lot of things, including not just how the teams will function, but how the leadership and management will adjust to their new roles.

Be aware, however, that when you do this type of incremental transformation, tension can occur between the team operating in the new framework and the other groups who are still in the old structure/mindset. This is one of the reasons why having a Change Leadership Team (CLT) in place is so helpful. All these elements work together to help the organization manage the transformation.

Now that we've looked at the way teams will work and be managed in the new framework, the next section will go into more details and tools for managing the change and staying out of the pitfalls.

UNLOCKING MOMENTUM – THE PROCESS

CHAPTER 8

SETTING UP FOR CHANGE: ALIGN FOR SUCCESS

TIMELINE: 0–6 MONTHS

When I talk about alignment here, I'm referring to several dimensional aspects that will all factor into the outcome. A lot of thoughtful planning and good communication go into this phase.

Figure 8.1 The Phases of Transformation

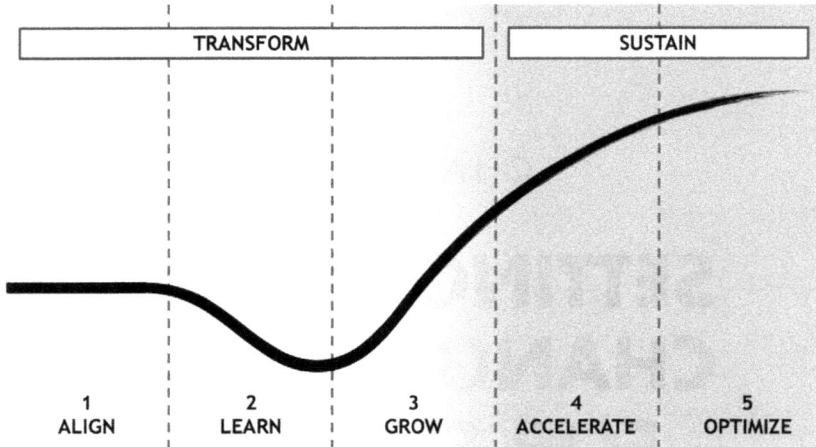

Each business transformation generally goes through five phases: Align, Learn, Grow, Accelerate, and Optimize. These phases never end, continuing to cycle through each new iteration of change. The black line J curve represents typical productivity/effectiveness during these stages, beginning as status quo, then dipping, and then rising to far higher rates than the starting point.

Invariably, when someone tells me their Agile transformation didn't work, and I dig into what happened, I can almost always trace the problem back to this phase and how they started off on the wrong foot. In fact, over my decades of working with clients of all different sizes and industries, I've observed that if you don't get this part right, you'll almost certainly be fated to go down one of those undesirable roads.

I'll give you more information on some of these pitfalls a little later in this and the next two chapters, but for now, let's talk about some of the key elements to ensure you get off on the right foot.

KEY PRINCIPLES AND COMMITMENTS

To start this transformation, you'll need to use or develop the following elements:

- An iterative approach using Agile methods
- An intentional organizational change management model focused on safety, engagement, and transparency
- Active leadership engagement to lead the change as role models for others
- Vision and goals: Obtain agreement to focus on a singular organizational optimizing goal
- Commitment: Avoid shiny objects
- A long-term view to ensure you don't declare victory too soon

Let's look at each of these things in more detail and examine why they're so essential.

AN AGILE-BASED, ITERATIVE APPROACH

Keep in mind that your transformation, even if it is focused on a single area or target within AgileOS®, such as Leaders, will be iterative; you will never really be finished, per se. This is a journey of continuous improvement, so you'll just go on to another cycle of transformation and improvement.

In addition, if you're implementing or anticipating multiple transformation initiatives, you'll probably have several in different phases. There's no "finished" here.

You'll always find another element to work on next, based on your current needs and priorities. Thus, it's not a "transformation project." There's no deadline by which everything will be completed. You may have certain goals, but they're not projects that end.

Figure 8.2 The Expanded AgileOS®

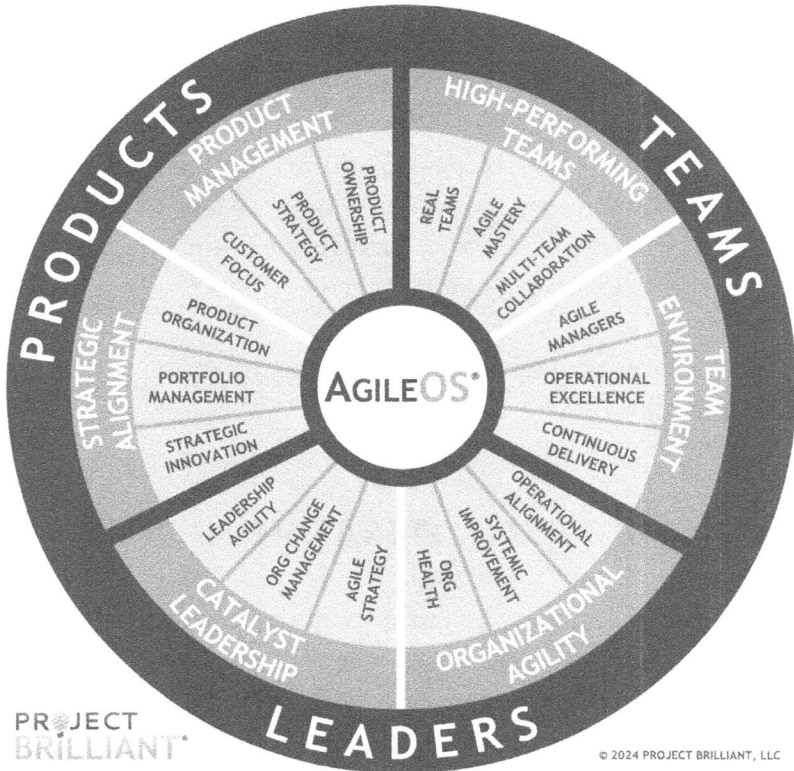

This diagram depicts the deeper aspects underlying the domains and subsections under Leaders, Products, and Teams. When transforming a business or an area, we go deeper into each area, refining subsections of those elements through different iterations of transformation based on the optimizing goal.

USE INTENTIONAL CHANGE MANAGEMENT MODELS

Well-established change management models will facilitate your transformation by helping you address and even prevent some potential barriers beforehand — especially those that are related to people.

For instance, let's begin with you.

Not to put you in the hot seat, but it's important to take inventory of your attitude and knowledge about leading and managing change. How familiar are you with doing it successfully? What is your knowledge in this area? Most importantly, what assumptions do you, or others in your company, hold that could hamper your success? Let's get those out of the way right off the bat.

Common False Assumptions about Change Management

People — and I'm not just talking about you — often believe change management is something it's not.

Here are some common assumptions we often see:

- Change management is just cheerleading for the change. All I need to do is be positive about it and keep encouraging people.
- Change management is just about communicating out to the people, like an email campaign.
- Change management is necessary only at the beginning; once the change is in place, we don't need to do it anymore.

- Change management is simple; it just involves creating new processes and having everyone learn and start following them.
- Change management just requires having a new vision and communicating that to everyone. But the vision will speak for itself; once exposed to it, everyone will see why it's good and how to achieve it.
- Change management is an external process in which leaders get a team, group, or whole organization to do something new.

These are just a few. Note that some might even be true in part, but they depict an incomplete view that doesn't address the whole situation.

The problem is that these assumptions often lead companies to do rudimentary change management, thinking that's enough, or they skip it altogether and just expect everything to go well. Neither of these expectations is realistic.

Successful change management requires leading the entire shift not only in vision, process, methods, and skills, but also in the organizational culture, including everyday assumptions, mindsets, and emotional aspects. Based on that premise, the problem with the above assumptions is that:

- They focus on a superficial level without addressing the deeper, more holistic aspects needed for true change, including people's mindsets, knowledge, and understanding levels, as well as the culture aspects.
- They assume the change is temporary — that once they "get there," they're finished worrying about it.

- They don't involve anyone else in creating the change. It's decreed from "on high," or wherever it's originating from, and it's just expected to happen from there.

Remember: You're shifting into a new mindset where change is not a time-boxed, one-time anomaly. Rather, it will be embedded continually into all your operations forever onward.

With that in mind, the above perspectives are a death sentence for the permanent, ongoing situation you're planning for. They reflect the very command-control management mindset that you're trying to get out of. How can you achieve your transformation by starting out in the same old way?

You can't.

Instead, we need a different way of thinking, one that addresses the whole set of needs. To do this, we use two powerful change models in tandem. **These support both the internal and external facets** that are equally vital for success.

Leading Change from Within: ADKAR

You can use whatever internal change management model you like, and we use several. One we really like is developed by the change management company Prosci.

It's called ADKAR, and the acronym stands for five components an individual needs to achieve successful change: awareness, desire, knowledge, ability, and reinforcement.

Prosci founder Jeff Hiatt's observations of change patterns of more than 700 organizations led to the development of this model, which helps individuals navigate change more successfully by addressing their own specific needs.

"Organizational changes often fail because employees don't understand the importance of getting on board the change or how to successfully make the change," the Prosci website notes. "They simply understand that a change is happening. And leaders are often not equipped to engage individuals effectively during the change and to manage any potential resistance."[21]

As I mentioned, you may have another model for internal change that you like better. That's fine. The most important factor is that you have a model in place for addressing internal elements such as resistance, fear, or lack of knowledge or understanding. The tools should help you gauge the emotional and mental aspects through client and employee surveys, focus groups, and other qualitative feedback gathering, and they should also make everyone feel included and safe in expressing their concerns.

Managing Change Externally: Kotter's 8-Step Model

You'll also need to have a model for addressing the external dimensions of the transformation. Much of what we do when we help our clients' business transformations adheres to an excellent model for leading change developed by John Kotter. It involves eight steps[22]:

1. **Create urgency for the transformation:** This will depend a little on your context, which we'll go into in the next section.

2. **Form a group to guide the change:** This is your Change Leadership Team or CLT.
3. **Set up your vision and strategy:** Again, this will also depend upon your context.
4. **Rally others to the cause:** Depending on your context, you'll want to determine who your allies are — not just strategically necessary peers, but also those most excited about the transformation.
5. **Remove obstacles:** Start addressing your internal and external barriers, including the mindsets and assumptions preventing progress.
6. **Celebrate short-term wins:** Keep morale and confidence high by continually setting up success in short-term increments.
7. **Build momentum:** Be prepared for situations when attention and/or enthusiasm wane.
8. **Reinforce the change:** Continually ensure the "new normal" is instilled throughout the organization and old habits/methods are left behind.

Again — this isn't the only model we use, and it's just a suggestion. The main point is that you need to lead the transformation through both the internal and external dimensions. This approach is much likelier to succeed than doing things from a singular or ad hoc mentality.

One more note: When you're leading change, you need a culture of safety. People need to feel comfortable suggesting solutions, making mistakes (which are learning experiences), and giving feedback or speaking up about problems. Without that culture, your teams won't be empowered to succeed.

Now that you're prepared with a change management model that includes the internal and external aspects, let's start engaging the right people. First, we'll need to look at the context a little more, as that will affect how to go about this part.

LEADERSHIP ENGAGEMENT: WHAT'S YOUR SITUATIONAL CONTEXT?

When you're preparing for your transformation, no matter where you want to start changing something, you will need to involve your leadership team first. This isn't only about getting buy-in and understanding, though those are obviously crucial. You also need to think from the standpoint of engaging them to do what's needed to make the change successful. It's about leading, as leaders.

So, your first hurdle may be based on where they are already in relation to their existing knowledge, commitment, and willingness to take part in the change. Based on our experience, that could vary between two distant sides of a spectrum:

- Your leadership is all-in: They've already embraced the need to transform the whole organization, and they want you to lead that change or be deeply involved; or
- You see the need for change to more adaptive operations, at least within your department or to solve a particular issue, and you want to pitch it to your leadership and relevant allies to make it happen.

Which position is more like yours?

Here's another important question. We've already talked about it, but you'll need a handle on it here.

What's your own mindset?

If you're in the first situation where your leadership is already convinced, it may be a little less pressure on you, but still, you could be wondering whether or not you're ready to commit to a long process of change. And you might wonder whether you can do it.

These are fairly common concerns, and I'm not going to tell you that it'll be easy. What I will tell you, though, is that, barring a catastrophe you have no control over, you will succeed if you are smart about what you're doing, use the right tools and practices, and commit to seeing it through.

If you're in the second situation where you're thinking about pitching the change, you might be thinking something like, "I don't know if I should put my neck on the line. What if the whole thing fails? Then it's me in the hot seat."

This worry is also common, and I understand it. You can feel like you're in a catch-22 situation. Leadership needs to see how it will work before they want to do it, but for them to see how it works, you need to do it. You might even feel that way, too — maybe you're thinking of trying it as an experiment and seeing what happens. Frankly, that's smart. It's reasonable to want to project a potential ROI before taking a bigger risk.

And, while you're thinking about risk, don't forget to ask whether you can risk *not* doing it. Sometimes that doesn't occur to people in these situations.

As we explored before, think about the opportunity cost: Where will business management practices be in five years? And what will your company look like in comparison? Looking back at the evolution of management practices, we saw that the companies that adopted practices that gave them advantages of efficiency/speed and better quality were better equipped to succeed. What do you think happened to the companies that didn't adopt these new practices right away? They would have been at a distinct disadvantage.

Business agility is the next stage of management evolution. The shift is already happening in the market, like it or not. If all your competitors have achieved fully adaptive operations within five years and you haven't, what happens to you? They'll be able to respond to market shifts faster; anticipate new needs; make quicker, more frequent improvements; and all the other benefits of being fully Agile.

So, can you risk potentially falling behind? As a leader, do you want to see your company succeed over the longer term? Would you like to feel you contributed to that success? How would it feel looking back five years from now, knowing you helped spearhead the next evolution for your company? Based on what my clients tell me, I'm betting it would feel pretty good.

Regardless of which situation you're in — whether or not leadership is on board (yet) — you'll still have a strong role to play. The first concern is how you'll work with leadership to solidify their commitment and move forward.

SOLIDIFYING ENGAGEMENT WHEN LEADERSHIP IS ALREADY ON BOARD

An ideal set of circumstances would be the first one: Your CEO and your entire executive leadership team are already all-in to restructure the entire company operations from a business agility perspective, rebuilding from the ground up. They either want you to help lead this charge, or they want you to play a key role, which might be why you're reading this book.

We've seen this happen in multiple ways, and it usually happens more with small to mid-size organizations that don't have to deal with the complexity of larger organizations.

For instance, we recently worked with a bank that employed around 250 individuals. They wanted to transform their entire organization and started with that commitment in mind. Then, they broke down that transformation goal, starting with a couple of smaller areas to see how it would work.

After they got their feet wet that way, they jumped in full force. So, though they did start with the smaller focus, they knew upfront that they were going to be doing the whole thing.

What You'll Still Need to Do

The planning for this situation happens differently from the incremental planning process when you're still testing the waters. In this situation, there's a lot more participation by leadership from the very beginning, and you can skip some of the steps of selling the idea. However, that doesn't mean you're ready to move forward.

You'll still need to do some things to ensure everyone is on the same page with what you're all about to do.

Ensure everyone accepts the depth of involvement. Make sure to eliminate any false assumptions that could be lurking under the surface. Everyone needs to be aware of the required amount of their involvement and what they'll need to be doing during the process. They may have bought into the idea, but that doesn't mean they totally understand what it will mean in terms of their own participation. The more involved and aligned they are with the change, the greater your chance of succeeding. This isn't a time when your leadership can just wave their hand at you and say, "Make it so." They have to be part of the change, too.

It will vary, but consider that many leaders need to clear, say, ten hours a week to have the appropriate availability. Don't just add to your plate; make sure you remove or delegate some of your workload. The last thing you want to do is further bury yourself and not be able to follow through on your commitments here. The entire organization is relying on leaders to lead this — don't let them down.

> **It will vary, but consider that many leaders need to clear, say, ten hours a week to have the appropriate availability.**

Ensure that everyone in leadership is clear about their roles. Usually, one or two individuals are set up to spearhead the change and will likely oversee the CLT (more on that in a moment). But how will the rest of leadership participate in the change? For instance, the CEO may take the stance of leading the culture shift aspect, while others may take on aspects such as changes in policy or organizational design once barriers are identified. This needs to be a team effort at the top, too. And remember what it takes to be a real team — dedication, commitment, and a common goal!

GETTING COMMITMENT WHEN YOU'RE PITCHING THE CHANGE

While having a leadership team that's already at least partly or fully committed to a transformation is nice, it's not as common as the scenario in which you'll need to get a commitment to participate from at least some people, and likely your CEO. Even if you've been asked to explore this route by your CEO, you'll still need to pitch it as a viable option and convince others to take on the goals.

If you skip this stage because your initiative is smaller and you don't feel you need to inform senior leadership, the results could be disastrous — you'll learn more in the following chapter about what happened to one group that made this mistake.

The following are some tips for what to do when you're working with the leadership team and other key stakeholders.

Pitch the change upfront, as soon as possible. In this scenario, it's important for the person who wants to lead the change at whatever level, even if it's just within their own department, to get the relevant commitments before starting. Don't wait, even if it's a change only in your own area. I'll talk more about that in a moment.

Get initial feedback. You'll need to be prepared for their questions, objections, and concerns. This is the time to field those, rather than wait till you're already underway to learn about them. The earlier you know how they feel about the project, the more you can proactively address any concerns or objections. They'll also feel heard, which helps soften the frustration when things don't go as well as they'd like.

Remember, your goal is to lead the charge, transforming incrementally to help others see the benefits over time. Getting initial commitments to participate is just the first step in a bigger process.

If you handle this set of steps well, what usually happens is that the first change becomes a template for the way other areas in the organization can do a similar transformation. Eventually, the entire organization will find itself having gone through the transformation without having planned to do so from the start (though a more concrete plan to do so usually emerges somewhere during the process once everyone has been convinced of the benefits).

ESTABLISH YOUR CHANGE LEADERSHIP TEAM (CLT)

I won't go into a lot of detail here since I've already described the function of the CLT in Chapter 5. This is just a reminder to establish your Change Leadership Team up front. These people will play a crucial role in making things transparent for everyone else, as well as putting in place all the rest of the parts needed to succeed. What that looks like depends on your organizational needs and the organizational change management models the CLT is using.

DETERMINE THE VISION AND GOALS

Obviously, your parameters depend on your transformational context — whether a holistic, full organizational change or one targeted to a single area or a specific problem.
Here are some components you'll need to consider:

Decide What You're Optimizing For

Organizations going through a transformation need to determine upfront what they want to achieve. We usually look at nine different potential optimizing goals (shown here in alphabetical order):

1. Continuous improvement
2. Customer satisfaction
3. Employee engagement
4. Innovation
5. Market responsiveness
6. Predictability
7. Productivity
8. Quality
9. Speed

What you choose will determine how you approach the components within your transformation initiative. In addition, if you're trying to optimize for two things at once, you'll find they conflict with each other. It's, therefore, important to select one and then commit to it. What you select should also reflect and be supported by your corporate values and mission (and if not, these may need to change, too), so choose wisely.

Determine Your Product Portfolio (Org-Wide)

If you're doing your full organizational transformation, you'll want to do this at the start. Conduct a workshop with your leadership team to determine your products. When we lead these workshops, they are often several-day, intensive events. It's best to do them offsite, away from your normal business space.

Create Your Future-State Map

This will depend on your goal. If you're transforming your whole organization, you'll be thinking from the top level to do this part.

You'll want to map your future state according to the products you have determined. This will be another intensive event, and again, it's best to do it offsite.

When we lead these exercises, we tell clients to forget about the current state and just focus on the future. Just start with a blank page and design the company the way you want it. Don't think about what you're doing at the moment — think about what you *should* be doing. What you're doing now doesn't matter for this part, and including it can actually interfere with your vision.

Think about it this way: It's like going from a caterpillar to a butterfly. Are you going to spend all your time thinking about why you're a caterpillar, or are you going to just stop being a caterpillar and start working on being a butterfly? This is also a good analogy because there's a dormant time when the transformation is happening. Nobody expects the caterpillar to be out doing caterpillar things while it's becoming a butterfly. When it's halfway there, it needs to just keep going. It also shouldn't be expected to come out of its cocoon and start doing butterfly things before it's finished transforming.

Decide to be a butterfly and start mapping out what the world looks like when you're a butterfly. Then start going there.

DECIDE ON YOUR FIRST TARGET AREA(S) AND PARAMETERS

This is where things can diverge depending on the context. However, it boils down to some iteration of change within the Leaders, Products, and Teams areas within AgileOS®, according to what you're trying to optimize for.

What is the ultimate goal for your organization? Are you trying to optimize for speed? Responsiveness to market? Innovation? You can only pick one. When you answer this question, you'll be surprised at how the answer simplifies how you evaluate your operations.

If you're transforming the whole organization, you might just start on the most important product based on your future-state model and go from there. You could spin up a parallel organization within your company and move some staff there to be on its team. That organization would operate within its own parameters and policies, which would happen independently of the others within the company.

However, you could do things differently based on an organizational goal. For instance, Perry's company had a specific business goal to change over to a new system. However, they set up that goal as a transformation exercise for the leadership and the teams.

The migration had some characteristics of a waterfall project in that they had a start and finish date for the system setup itself. What they transformed was the way they handled the data migration and setup. Instead of doing it in the regular way, they used it to train their teams in Scrum methods. They treated the system itself as an internal product, as it served (and added value to) many of the groups that handled the company's products. By revamping how leadership was handling the oversight and how the teams worked together to do the transfer, their transformation focused on the Teams and Leaders segments of the AgileOS® system. The teams then continued to maintain the system as the rest of the company began transforming other areas.

Whatever you decide to do, just remember that it will create benefits no matter how small or large it is.

Avoid Common Budgeting Mistakes

One of the most common mistakes companies make when using the incremental approach is managing the budget as if it's a waterfall project with a start and finish date. When the initial transformation is finished, they suddenly realize there's no more money set aside to support ongoing efforts.

This budget gap can cause them to start falling back into old models as they scramble to keep the new situation afloat. Even in the best cases, the recovery time creates lags. The worst case is when the initial effort succeeds, but the lack of resources forces them to simply abandon it. This is a morale-killer that can linger for years, coloring the perceptions of everyone involved.

If you're spinning up a parallel organization, think about its budget as an ongoing factor and plan it based on supporting your value-delivery goals versus how it's always been done. You could plan it in small increments versus annually, or even as a budget stream based on need, versus having a "plan."

SETTING UP YOUR TEAM AND MANAGEMENT

To achieve your desired future state, consider who you will be shifting where. Determine this during the Align phase.

Remember: The roles and expectations will be changing, both for the teams and for the managers, and it's really not possible to shift one without the other. Therefore, you'll need to plan not only how the teams will function, but also how your managers will start working mentally toward their new roles.

We've discussed this during the Teams overview in previous chapters, so I won't go into great detail here. However, one tip: Choose people based on their knowledge, skill sets, and excitement about the transformation. Don't make the mistake of picking people just because they have nothing to do.

When you set up the team, make sure to also choose how the management will be configured. Your Scrum master, product owner, and the rest should all be determined based on the value-delivery criteria and their knowledge levels and interest at the same time you're designing your team (preferably, with their participation).

BEWARE OF BAILOUT MOMENT #1: THE SHINY OBJECT DISTRACTION

Working with so many clients over the years, as well as just watching what happens in the industry, we've identified several points during the process where clients get distracted by something else, immediately losing all their forward progress on the transformation. For example, maybe a new market opportunity arises, and those leading the transformation would need to seize the opportunity. That could be a great opportunity, especially in the short term. But does it get you where you need to go for the long term in the same way the transformation does? That's up to you to decide, but just be aware that you're no longer transforming; you're continuing the status quo.

Figure 8.3 The Shiny Object Distraction

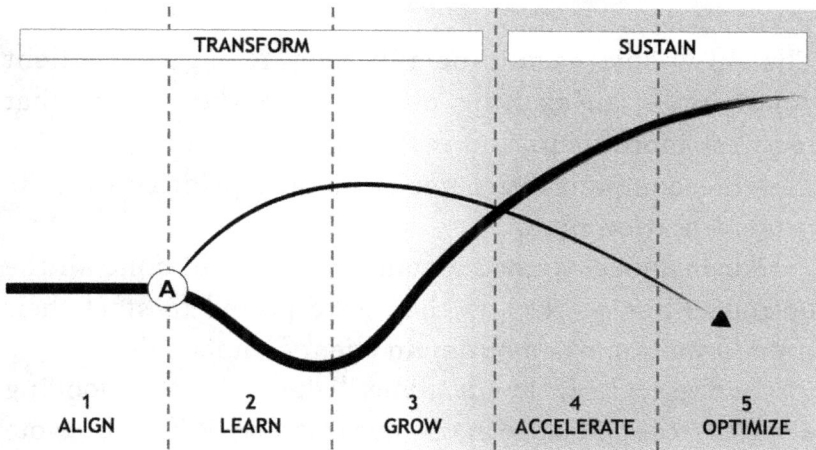

There are several points at which an organization's path can deviate from the standard expected curve. The first point can occur when the organization is through the Align phase but then becomes distracted and pursues a different goal, usually focused on a short-term gain such as chasing a new customer or a different major initiative.

In Figure 8.3, the main line is a J curve illustrating a normal transformation, in which the business begins at a flat-line status quo where the Align phase begins. Then there's a drop in productivity, after which everything bottoms out, and the situation rebounds with enormous gains in productivity — far surpassing what the organization did before.

You can also see that there's another line that deviates at Point A, right after everything is finished with the Align phase. In this situation, the company has its plan and is about to "jump off the cliff" into the Learn and Grow phases to make it happen when, suddenly, it gets hit with what we call a shiny object.

What Shiny Object?

The shiny object could be anything. A huge new client opportunity, an exciting merger, a market uptick that requires more focus and resources — anything positive that the company feels needs to take priority over its transformation plan.

For instance, we had a company that had done all the upfront Align work, and they were poised to start their transformation when our main client contact called.

"We've got a big new customer!" she said. "We're looking at a 20 percent increase in revenue this year. We can't devote the time and money toward the transformation. We're going to need to shift all our resources toward serving this new client instead." This was the decision of the CEO/owner.

So, they took on the new customer and essentially canceled their transformation. They did see an uptick in revenue in the short term; it was a good market opportunity. But twelve months later they were back to wondering how to improve and once again realizing their status quo approach wasn't getting them ahead. That temporary revenue boost did nothing to help them in the long term.

The moral here is that when you make this commitment, really make it. Burn the boats. There's no going back.

HEADING INTO THE NEXT PHASE

Alignment usually takes around six months, but it can be more or less depending on the variables of your first step, including the complexity and size of the initiative.

When you've done everything and set up your first team, you're ready to head into the following two phases: Learn and Grow. Let's move into the next chapter and look at what happens in those.

CHAPTER 9

BUILDING MOMENTUM: LEARN & GROW

TIMELINE: 3-12 MONTHS

The next two phases, Learn and Grow, set the transformation in motion. I jokingly call this the "jumping off the cliff" phase because it's a test of faith to start. You're jumping from one mode into another totally different mode, and that can be unsettling — though probably not as life-threatening as cliff jumping.

FOCUS AREAS DURING THE LEARN AND GROW PHASES

When you head into these phases, you'll be focused on the following elements:

- Continuing change leadership
- Training and skills development
- Metrics and assessment of progress
- Addressing internal stakeholders' concerns
- Communicating the short-term wins
- Managing for the new situation
- Removing barriers to progress

Let's look further into how to approach these elements for the best results.

CONTINUING CHANGE LEADERSHIP

During these phases, we'll be focused on all facets of the internal and external change management models you've selected. In fact, from now on, you'll be using these in some way throughout this iterative process. Each time you enter a new transformation cycle in response to a market change or other reason, or whenever you choose to work on a new initiative related to your main optimization goal (productivity, speed, innovation, etc.), you'll need to pull out the appropriate tools.

For instance, when you're jumping off the cliff, people are going to be excited and scared. People aren't going to know what to do, and they'll be worried about making mistakes or looking/feeling stupid, among many other concerns.

Leaders will need to be mindful of staying in their new roles — coaching, but not getting in the way. Letting teams work out their solutions themselves. Everyone will need to be aware of what's going on, so transparency will be crucial. All of these will factor in with each of the following components for the Learn phase.

TRAINING YOUR TEAM(S)

This training period focuses on training the leaders, teams, and managers in Agile methodologies and roles. In addition, during this phase, your team will also be building its own culture and focus areas, as well as internal relationships around the new value-delivery goals.

Top-Level Agile Training Tips

Here are some things that will help ensure your training achieves its goals.

Require all relevant people to attend, and train them all at once. Everyone related to the first area of transformation needs to attend the training. I know this isn't always feasible with smaller teams who are also still handling crucial support roles, so do the best you can in this respect.

Also, we often hear people say, "Oh, Susie doesn't need to come to the training — she's already trained in Scrum." That doesn't matter. For one thing, Susie may have trained elsewhere, and you don't know the quality or focus of her training. Every training is different. In addition, Susie trained with another team, not this one. Part of the training is bonding with the new team during the process. You need Susie to train with the team to get that shared experience.

Even when the team attends the same training, they can come out with mixed messages or mixed understanding. They need the immersive experience together to solidify not just Scrum and Agile but how to work together as well.

Provide adequate time for the training. When Project Brilliant does Scrum training, we have a two-week Team Liftoff period during which the first two days are focused on immersive, hands-on training. The rest of the time is spent preparing for the first Sprint with team building, team identity, refining the first work items we'll take on, and nailing down details of the team's collaboration and work process. Whenever we get pushback about the timeframe at the beginning, we stick to our guns. It needs to be a two-week period. We know this from solid experience. The initial two-week investment brings a 10x return. Afterward, we invariably get comments like, "Oh my God, I'm so glad you made us stick to the two weeks. This would have been much more difficult if we hadn't."

Include time for the team to reset their work approach. In this, have the team actually work as a Scrum team to start setting up their new processes, solve logistics issues, and think proactively about how they'll address their first Sprint.

Ensure the training is the only thing the relevant people are working on during that timeframe. Again, I'm aware this isn't always possible with crucial support roles, but try to minimize the situations where people don't have the opportunity to fully participate. Otherwise, they'll miss out on key learnings and the shared experience that will help them bond as a team. Without these elements, they'll make slower progress.

I definitely don't advise trying to do something like half-day training with the other half of the day spent doing regular things. That creates a weird situation where they're not really doing it the new way or the old way. It also waters down the effectiveness of the hands-on component, which is meant to get them into new habits asap.

Move forward without looking back. When the training is over, you're ideally now using the Agile-only methods. You're not going back into a hybrid situation or having teams who are doing both Agile and waterfall projects. Everyone is dedicated to the new way from here forward. Period. Have the team learn Agile by doing Agile and learn Scrum by doing Scrum. This is just as much about guiding the team to use Agile practices as it is about guiding management and leadership in their new roles. The team needs to start experiencing having autonomy and management's trust.

TRAINING LEADERSHIP AND MANAGEMENT

One of the funniest parts about the training phase is the way leadership and management react. They really, really hate to see things going poorly. They want to jump in and help.

This is, unfortunately, the worst thing they can do.

The whole point of the Liftoff period is to start shifting the authority for finding solutions to the team. Leadership and management can't try to fix everything for the team, or the team won't get to the point where they're taking ownership for themselves and achieving the productivity gains leadership wants to see.

Senior leadership can be sucked into this as easily as the management level. I've seen C-suite executives with worried expressions hovering around teams like helicopter parents, trying to help them fix a problem. The leader means well, but it doesn't help.

My son plays high school football. At the very first meeting of the parents, his coach told us, "If a problem or question arises, I do not want you to contact me. Part of my philosophy is to help your sons become adults and take responsibility for themselves. If they have an issue, they need to talk with their teammates. If it needs to be escalated, they are the ones who need to escalate it. If I'm hearing from you — the parents — things have gone very wrong in the chain of responsibility."

He's right. Parents are fans in the stands. Their job is watching and cheering. Not calling plays. Not determining the starting lineup. Not arguing with the refs. Let the team and coaches take care of playing the game.

With the Scrum teams, leadership and managers need to be fans in the stands.

The framework is established and proven. Even if it isn't working perfectly at the beginning, the teams will figure out how to fix it. They need everyone outside the team to get out of their way. If it seems counterintuitive at first, it will eventually start making sense as the team steps into their responsibilities.

ASSESSING PROGRESS

Speaking of leaders getting in the way, one of the other problems we see a lot is their expectations of what progress will look like. This is where the CLT can play a crucial role, as they can help manage realistic expectations.

Leadership and management are used to thinking of progress in bottom-line terms such as revenue and productivity. However, in this case, those numbers will be significantly lagging metrics and won't tell the whole story. Leaders need to be prepared for that.

First off, the teams themselves need to go through a set of formative phases, and where they are within those phases should be one metric showing progress or not.

Team Formation Progress

We measure the success of the team formation in terms of the Tuckman Model. In this, there are four phases:

- **Forming** (starts during Liftoff, typically 1–2 months) — the very beginning when the team is learning their roles and how they will work together.
- **Storming** (typically 2–3 months at earliest) — trying to work together while also dealing with clashes of ideas, differing perspectives and approaches, confusion on roles, and other

interpersonal conflicts. This is the trust-building phase, originating when people start to voice differing opinions and build alliances to solve problems.

- **Norming** (typically 3-6 months at earliest) — settling into reliable, productive behaviors and relying on/trusting each other as they continue improving their ability to meet the work expectations.
- **Performing** (typically 6 months at earliest) — achieving high productivity as they learn to anticipate and prevent problems, increase their efficiency and effectiveness, and become better at determining the best priorities and solutions for value delivery.[23]

Team Productivity

Be ready. Because team productivity will slow dramatically in the short term. This is inevitable, if for no other reason than during the two-week Liftoff, they won't be completing any work — they are learning a new way of working. And when they come out of that two-week Liftoff, they'll be playing a new game for the first time. It takes a few cycles to get into a new habit. This is the forming phase, and they need a little leeway to get going.

When you focus everyone on training in a completely new way, with a totally different group of people than they're used to working with, you're going to have a slow time. We've seen this on the J-curve, when everything bottoms out (see Fig. 9.1 as a reminder).

Figure 9.1 Temporary Low Productivity During Early Phases

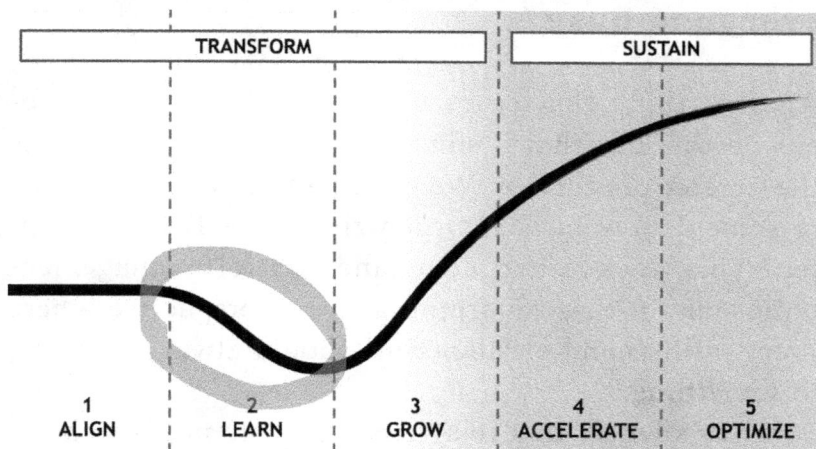

During the Learn phase and the beginning of the Grow phase, the productivity and effectiveness temporarily dip as the team must let go of its old ways and learn the new processes/methods.

I'm assuming you've anticipated and communicated this important fact ahead of time for the sake of transparency. However, even if everyone's prepared, when you get there, it can still be unsettling for some people. That's one of the main reasons why the helicopter parents come down from the stands and try to help. They just hate to see the team failing.

But remember: These are the Learn and Grow phases. Part of learning and growing is trying things and seeing what works and what doesn't. The team needs to have the room to do this. If everyone is freaked out because there's "no productivity," but the team is making huge strides toward fixing that, then you are still making progress.

Reminder: Productivity Is Not "Keeping Everyone Busy"

Another thing that crops up during this time is a focus on the idea that if someone isn't busy all the time, they aren't productive. We've already talked about this to some degree in the "Organizing True Teams" chapter. This is another command-control management philosophy focused more on a Lean perspective where every millisecond of labor time should always be going to something.

This is where that relay-race thinking needs to be in play. People will have some downtime while they're waiting for the baton. Overall, the goal is team effectiveness, not individual productivity. If you're focused too much on keeping the individual busy all the time, you'll hamper the team.

THE CLT: MANAGING STAKEHOLDER EXPECTATIONS

During this time, when people see the old productivity metrics going down, it's crucial for the CLT to stay engaged.

Preventing Panic When the Marble Is Missing

First off, business stakeholders need to know what's happening. Remember, we're in a Rube Goldberg scenario. Say there's a manager — we'll call her Sally — who, for the last ten years of her career, has been in charge of watching the Rube Goldberg marble roll by and measuring whether or not it was early or late, and how well it tipped the lever that made the bell ding, causing the rooster to crow, and so on.

Sally has dedicated years of her life to measuring how fast the marble sped by on its path and how loudly the bell dinged, and all kinds of other metrics about marbles and bells. She is so knowledgeable about marbles and bells that she even dreams about them at night sometimes.

And then, one day, Sally is watching her part of the machine, and the marble doesn't go by.

She waits, dumbfounded. And still...

Nothing.

This is horrible. What is going on? Has there been a catastrophe? Sally immediately panics and starts making phone calls. Her entire world seems to be crashing down. If there's no marble, what is she supposed to do?

She can't do her job without the marble.

The Rube Goldberg machine is predictable, even though it's crazy and unnecessarily complicated.

Even if the CLT communicated that this would happen, Sally didn't necessarily see the communication. She might have been too busy to read the newsletter. Maybe she wasn't in the meeting. Whatever the reason, she needs someone who can give her the information she needs to feel all right about not having a marble to measure for a while — maybe even for good. Because Sally's job of measuring marbles might change to measuring something else, hopefully, she'd already know that if the CLT was doing its job well.

Communicating Short-Term Wins

What did the team figure out with the new methods that no one had achieved in the old way? What are some things the last Sprint just achieved? How are decisions being made better now? There's more to success than the bottom line during this phase.

The CLT needs to communicate those things as they happen. The gains are reassuring to senior leadership and management, especially business stakeholders who worry their needs aren't being served by the group undergoing the change.

One client we've been working with in the healthcare industry had a situation where they had been trying to bring some strategic initiatives to fruition, but they'd gotten stalled. The main issue was that leadership was pressuring them to use waterfall methods to plan and predict everything, and that wasn't working. It was a huge plan, with a schedule involving more than 500 line items and dependencies. They kept going off the plan, and leadership was getting impatient.

We worked with them to reignite the teams and start working on these goals again. We had to guide them through a reset on being an Agile team with a two-week Team Liftoff, followed immediately by starting into two-week Sprints. As is typical, the first two Sprints were a little wonky in terms of getting actual work items accomplished while we adjusted things, so we didn't even show the executives what we'd built yet.

By the third Sprint, though, we invited the executives to see what was going on. And the first thing they did was freak out because, in their minds, we'd had eight weeks to make progress. That eight weeks consisted of Liftoff (training and team formation), the first two Sprints of learning how to really work together in a real Agile team, and then one Sprint of really starting to get things done well. And they looked back to the original plan, becoming concerned that we were already off schedule.

The solution was to communicate better about the progress we had made during those eight weeks, not just with the business goals but with the team formation. We weren't "there" yet, but we had moved forward on incremental aspects that were taking us to the long-term goal. We had several short-term wins we could talk about that made us optimistic about the long term.

This information gave leadership the confidence to stop trying to predict everything and just go with the flow, which allowed the team to focus on delivering the initiatives instead of trying to micromanage details.

After that third Sprint, the team started to really gel, and productivity doubled and tripled from what it had been prior to the reset. From there forward, the team was rocking, and the executives were certainly surprised at how far the team had come in just a few months. Not only did they recover the "lost time" (in the execs' eyes), but they also started to outpace the original scheduled pace within a few months.

The funny part was that the original plan called for five different major customer features, but the customers were actually so happy with the first three that the product manager realized the other two weren't really needed. They'd planned to spend the full budget on those, but then realized they could get happy customers and 80 percent of their expected ROI by only spending about 60 percent of what they had planned. Sticking to their original plan wasn't even necessary after all, from an ROI standpoint.

Ways to Communicate Goals and Short-Term Wins

You can measure your success both through your KPIs/outcome metrics and through your transformation metrics, which will show different types of success.

The KPIs and outcome metrics should show how the transformation is affecting your business. These metrics should ideally revolve around achieving your optimizing goal — one of the nine we discussed in the previous chapter, such as speed, quality, or innovation. If you're measuring general KPIs like billable hours, inventory turnover, or lobby wait time, it can be straightforward to compare the before and after of these to show how the transformation is affecting them over time. However, with a new process or a new optimizing goal, your KPIs may change, and you won't necessarily be comparing apples to apples. In these situations, you can still track your outcome metrics — for instance, customer satisfaction and how it increased after the transformation.

You can also show progress on the transformation itself. These metrics are more about how successful you are in changing people's mindsets, perceptions, engagement levels, and behaviors, or how you are adapting to new ways of working. What's improved since the last time you looked at this metric? How far along are you on the change curve?

To measure these things, you can use periodic employee surveys, behavioral observations, and other tools to take a "before" snapshot and then benchmark against that with the same type of measurement later. Even noticing things like how well the team performed as an Agile Scrum team, working together this time instead of working alone in their cubicles like they did last time, can illustrate incremental successes.

CONTINUE MANAGING FOR THE NEW SITUATION

After training and well through the Storming phase, everyone in a leadership or management role will need to be mindful to ensure the new roles are clear and that people don't fall into old habits.

For instance, one of the most common conflicts during the Storming phase is confusion between the product owner and the Scrum master. The product owner often thinks their title means they own the team. So, they try to manage the team — setting meetings, leading decisions on how to approach goals, etc. — but that's the Scrum master's job. The Scrum master is the team coach, while the product owner sets the customer priorities. These roles will need to be continually reinforced until everyone fully understands them.

People can also fall into old habits. Those used to functional isolation will just naturally start to go off and do their piece of the Sprint by themselves.

The Learn phase is much more about unlearning old ways than about layering new methods on top of what was always done. Keep this in mind as you're managing through the change.

Ideas for Ongoing Stakeholder Communication Tactics

If you're trying to come up with ways to communicate with the key stakeholders, here are some tactics that have worked for our clients.

Quarterly employee engagement survey reports. These are helpful for showing trends. One company's initial survey showed people weren't so confident. By the third survey, they saw the trendline moving up.

Monthly change management newsletter. Each month, one leader would highlight the goals for the upcoming month and the wins from the previous one. This ongoing progress report helped keep confidence high and momentum going.

Friday Week-in-Review. One CIO started putting out a really nice weekly email to the whole company highlighting the week's achievements, and also noting things that didn't go so well, that they weren't going to do again. It was a very simple format and quick read, only 2–3 paragraphs or so each time.

Sprint Review and Sprint forecasts. When the teams get more productive, they can start forecasting their progress ahead of time, predicting whether they're ahead or behind on the current goal. This helps leadership maintain confidence and also allows for better planning. You can also do multi-team Sprint Reviews, which are probably not quite what you'd expect. It's not each team taking their turn on the projector. Think of it more like a big science fair where leadership and management from different areas get to come walk around and see what everyone is doing. These are great for maintaining transparency and getting frequent feedback from broad sets of stakeholders.

These are the kinds of things leaders and managers can devote their time to in order to support their teams and their entire organization's success. If you're tempted to micromanage things, put that nervous energy toward something like this instead — your teams will thank you.

REMOVE INTERNAL BARRIERS TO PROGRESS

Sometimes, as leaders are planning during the Align phase, they start focusing too much on where they are now and seeing all the barriers, and it gets overwhelming.

That's why we don't want to focus on barriers until we start moving toward the first initiative. At that point, we're focused on that one goal, so we have much more clarity on what's really in the way at that moment. Sure, in the Rube Goldberg machine, everything's in the way of everything else, but those things aren't important at this particular moment.

By thinking in terms of the concrete goal and the barriers to it, you can prioritize removing those specific barriers — or working around them — first.

Common Internal Barriers

Most of the barriers teams encounter involve one or more of the following:

Counter-productive policies. We've discussed this a bit, but when you're training teams to think and operate as a team and your HR incentives are set up to reward only an individual, there's a disconnect. Some policies that can create barriers include those that specify how promotions, hiring/firing, pay raises, performance management, and other types of management considerations work. Other sets of policies that may create barriers are those related to your business office/budgeting and finance, risk management, information security, and so forth.

Systems limitations. If you're trying to do something like spin up a parallel organization, your current systems architecture and tools may not support the needs of the new group. Even if you're managing your teams in different ways, you may need to look at setting up some parallel systems specific to the new organization. Eventually, the rest of the company may shift over to the new systems as individual areas go through their transformation.

Regulatory considerations. Regulations can create obstacles to becoming Agile as well. If you originally documented your process to fulfill regulatory requirements, and it was based on a waterfall process, you have to stick to that process for audits. This creates a situation where you're trying to be Agile and waterfall at the same time, which doesn't work. It's fixable through re-documenting your process within your Agile framework. This can be a huge step for larger organizations or those with multiple documented processes, but if you truly want to be Agile, you really have to do it. You can't fully commit to Agile if you're beholden to an old waterfall audit process.

Friction between the team and those still working under the old paradigm. This can be significantly decreased with proper organizational support and change leadership, but it still happens. Ensuring communication channels are open between Agile and traditional teams is important, and management can take on this role to help facilitate that communication. Make sure you don't become the middle person — rather, encourage direct communication between the parties themselves.

Mental roadblocks. We've already talked about a lot of these, but they're worth mentioning here because they happen frequently. These mental blocks could be within team members themselves or anywhere throughout the organization. They show up as incorrect understanding of their roles, unproductive attitudes, waterfall thinking, rigid ideas, old work habits, lack of information on or understanding of expectations, fear of change or the unknown, or refusal to let go of individual heroism and become one with the team. When someone was really smart and valuable within the old way, and now you're trying to get them to be collaborative, share the glory, and be mentors to each other, they can balk.

Putting people into the wrong roles. We've discussed how leadership needs to use care when shifting people to new roles — for instance, I brought up the confusion some companies have when trying to find a place for traditional project managers in an Agile environment.

The best approach is to really understand the skill set and responsibilities of the new role options before moving someone into it (see Figure 9.2). The person might still need some training, but if they are interested in or excited about the focus of a new role, that's a great sign they'll put in the work to succeed.

If someone isn't performing well in a specific role despite more training or clarifying expectations, it's best to work with them to find a different role more suited to their interests and skills.

Figure 9.2 Analyzing Overlapping Skills with Different Roles

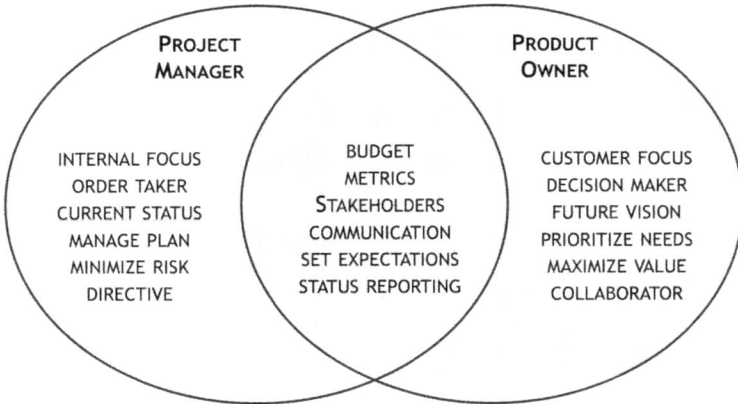

When deciding which new roles to move people into during the transformation, try to look at overlapping skill sets. For instance, the role of project manager from the old situation only has a few overlapping skills in relation to the product owner role in the new situation, as seen here. In this case, people from the current roles may or may not be a fit for the new role depending on what they are able to learn and whether they are interested in growing into the new role.

BEWARE OF PITFALLS #2–3: MORE BAILOUT MOMENTS

In the last chapter, we started looking at some of the most common times when clients suddenly change direction in mid-transformation. During the Learn/Grow phases, this can happen at two additional points. Let's look at those in order of how far down the road they typically happen.

Bailout Moment #2: Panicking Partway Down the Cliff

Figure 9.3 Panicking Partway Down the "Cliff"

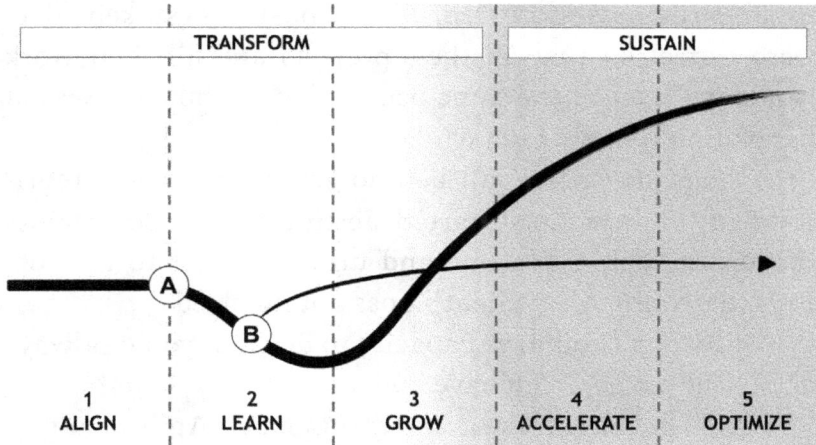

The second bailout point occurs at Point B, when the team has already "jumped off the cliff" and productivity levels start to dip. Seeing these lower levels or some other perceived cause for alarm, management gets nervous, potentially deciding to abandon the change and attempt to revert to the original status quo.

In Figure 9.3, you can see that Point B illustrates an exit point just as the drop in productivity begins.

In this situation, the company has its plan, has "jumped off the cliff" into the Learn and Grow phases, and then, either because they're seeing the productivity drop or for some other reason, they bail out.

A good example of this was a company that had some middle-tier managers who wanted to go through the transformation to Agile. They were confident they could do it, and because it only involved their own departments, they were certain their leadership didn't care as long as they were still achieving results.

We got through the Align phase and into Learn; their teams were working on different projects. But then the usual situations occurred. Their business stakeholders were expecting that all their projects and all their work would get done at the same pace as before, but that wasn't happening reliably for a while.

Things started to fall behind schedule or were reprioritized. Stakeholders started getting upset. Complaints ran up the chain of command until they got to the top. Eventually, the main client's boss got involved.

"Why don't you have capacity to do what you've always done?" he asked. "You have budget."

"Well, because we're going through this Agile change," the manager tried to explain. But by that point, it was too late. They hadn't been communicating all along, so there was no context for anything, nothing to show any benefits. All the leadership team saw was that the groups weren't performing as they expected. That was what they cared about.

There's always a point during the decision phase in Align when you have to ask, "Are we willing to take that short-term hit for the long-term benefit?" The time to agree on that is before you start.

But now, these guys were forced to ask that question after they'd started down the road. And because they had already missed their opportunity to communicate and inform their leadership, the answer was no.

So, they'd already jumped off the cliff, but it was a false start. They scrambled to get to a ledge on the cliffside, and then they had to climb back up, taking more time and resources to get to the place they'd been before. All their planning time and effort was wasted, and morale suffered, too.

The moral of this story is: if you're not committed, don't jump. It's that simple. Otherwise, you risk spending the time, effort, and money getting ready for the jump, only to pull the plug and waste it all just to continue on the previous status quo path... but with a lower level of morale and increased skepticism about any future change initiatives.

Point C: House on Fire

Figure 9.4 Running from a House on Fire

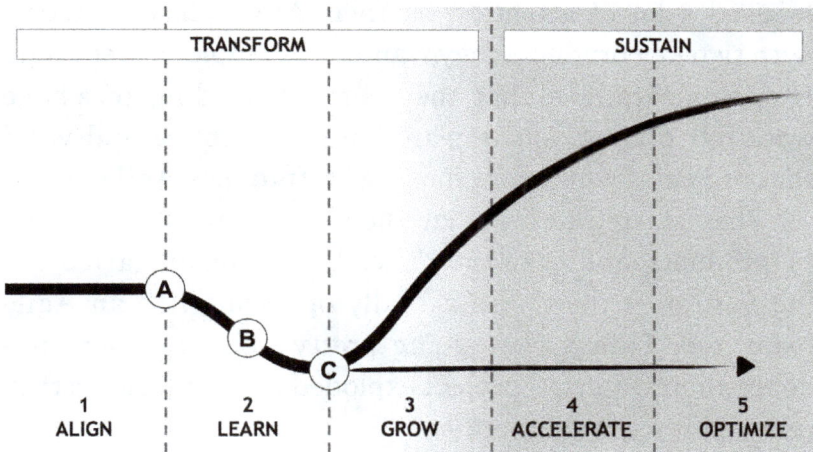

The final point at which organizations often abandon their business transformation occurs at the lowest point on the J curve, shown at Point C here, and is usually precipitated by a catastrophic event of some kind. Because the company doesn't stay with the transformation plans, it never experiences the accelerated growth of the Accelerate and Optimize phases and can often flatline at the bottom, well below its previous status quo.

Now, let's look at the last point where organizations falter. This one is the worst. Companies rarely recover from it.

In this situation, a company gets to Point C, and they've bottomed out on their J-curve (see Figure 9.4). They're just about ready to start rebounding upward when something devastates them, leaving the transformation flatlined at the bottom. It takes them years to recover from it, if they ever do.

Almost always, the issue goes back to mistakes they've made in the Align phase. It usually relates to trying to do too much at once, not realizing the resources they'll need for their transformation, and underestimating the commitment of time and budget to recover up the curve.

One of our larger clients, a medical device company, focused a lot of attention on their Align phase, starting with two key products they wanted to completely redesign. However, parallel to that, they were also working on a huge waterfall project. Their plan was to complete and wind that project down before moving staff to new Agile teams.

They started to organize their teams by their internal IT products, and even the IT leadership team started doing Scrum — they were actually operating like an Agile team, too. Things were going pretty well, and then suddenly, their waterfall project exploded in their faces as they released it to production.

They'd taken a lot of risk when they launched it, and they didn't have a proper backup plan for when things went bad. They didn't have anything to revert back to. It took them months to fix, and it took down their entire production assembly line. They couldn't sell anything for months and lost hundreds of millions of dollars in lost and delayed orders. They had to completely abandon everything they were doing, moving people from nearly every department to keep production moving at all. That also meant aborting their Agile transformation. It was all hands on deck to fix the broken IT system.

Obviously, this catastrophe had nothing to do with their Agile transformation. Even without trying to start on Agile at the same time, they probably would have had the same issues with the waterfall project due to the way it was implemented.

However, it's an interesting case study because it shows how risky big-bang waterfall projects can be. And with such a huge project still underway, they needed to have backup plans in place regardless of whether they were starting forward on Agile. I'm not sure if they skimped on that aspect due to their focus on Agile or not.

Most importantly, however, it illustrates how quickly a waterfall project can snowball into an avalanche. It's just one more reason to change to Agile methods, which can help prevent regular problems from quickly becoming catastrophes. If they had implemented that new system using Agile methods, it might not have gone so widely off track. We'll never know, but it's something to think about.

THE PITFALLS AREN'T THE NORM

Honestly, when you follow the right practices, pitfalls like this are the exception rather than the norm. In fact, they usually only occur when you don't do things right. Of our clients, only a small percentage bail out in this way. Most move along through their transformation at their own pace, learning and growing along the way, without ending in catastrophe.

I'm mainly singling these cases out to show you why it's so important to include the correct steps in your process. Whenever you hear stories about things not going well, it's most likely because those implementing the change skipped steps or didn't follow thorough change leadership practices. It's just like anything else. When you don't do this all the time, it's easy to overlook things.

THE NEXT PHASE: MOVING UPWARD

Now that you've worked your way through the Learn and Grow phases, let's move forward into the last two phases, Accelerate and Optimize. This is where things start to get a little easier and more fun, and you start seeing the productivity increases you've been aiming for.

CHAPTER 10

MAINTAINING LONG-TERM MOMENTUM: ACCELERATE & OPTIMIZE

So, you've aligned your organization around the new goals, set up your teams, and made it through the Forming and Storming phases. Now, you're starting to take off. Your teams have entered Norming, and they are hitting their stride. Sprints are going better and better. You're on the upswing in the J-curve, and you've pushed through any challenges that could have caused you to bail out prematurely. What happens now?

You keep going as if you haven't really achieved the goal. The goal was to start down a path that doesn't end. So once you're on the path, you've achieved the goal — you've replaced the mindset of start-to-finish end goals (projects) with a journey of ongoing transitions to new levels of value and quality (products). The journey doesn't ever really end.

ANTICIPATE THE NEXT J-CURVE(S)

There's not just one.

In fact, to get an idea of what this journey will be like, take a look at Figure 10.1.

Figure 10.1 The Ongoing, Ever-Improving Transformation

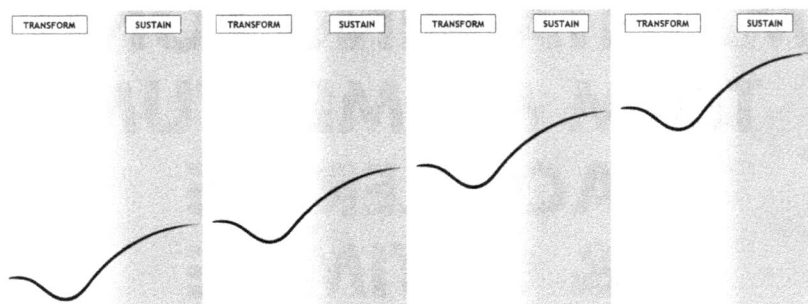

Because the business has adopted intentional change as its new practice, the change curve for the first iteration will level off, and then new change will bring the next curve. The goal is for each leveling-out phase to be higher in productivity, effectiveness, and resilience (thus also likely higher in things such as profitability and sustainability) than the last.

As you can see, the road ahead is filled with never-ending repetitions of these J-curves. That means you'll not only need to have the metaphoric equivalent of sport suspension and good tires (which I do advise), but you'll also be climbing each time. Each new level of productivity will get higher, and each "bottoming out" spot will be higher than the last, too. (If you bottom out while doing a Dukes of Hazzard jump in the wrong car, it's not my fault. I tried to warn you.)

This is what you're moving into. You're on the right road, and your target destination is the journey itself.

WHAT TO FOCUS ON DURING THESE PHASES

When you get to the Accelerate and Optimize phases, your main responsibility as a leader is to maintain your role as a catalyst leader to help the organization achieve greater business agility now that the base values have been instilled.

During these phases, you'll be working on the following:

- Reinforce everything you've done in the Align, Learn, and Grow phases.
- Avoid the pitfall of limited temporary agility.
- Refine some of the higher-level aspects of the AgileOS® framework, such as portfolio management and organizational health.
- Refine your skills as a catalyst leader.

Let's explore some of this in more depth.

AGILITY IS ITERATIVE

One of the most beneficial aspects of thinking from an Agile perspective is that you are no longer mired in linear, waterfall thinking. Instead, you've unlearned this type of thinking.

Therefore, as you move into each phase, you're not proceeding in a succession of one-two-three steps in which you must first complete Step 1, then leave it behind as you progress to Step 2, and so on. Instead, your new phases each contain small parts of Steps 1, 2, and 3 simultaneously. As you move to a new phase, you add more parts of the old Steps 1, 2, and 3 and perhaps also a Step 4, which you could never get to. Each time, you're embedding all the necessary aspects into that particular phase.

With this in mind, with each iterative phase of your development, your organization is always practicing aspects of the Align, Learn, and Grow phases. In fact, only when you're continuing to do all of the Align, Learn, and Grow activities well can you evolve to the Accelerate and Optimize phases. They aren't really timeline phases; they're measurements of how well you're expressing the values of Agile thinking.

During every Sprint, the teams are thinking about modifying their next plan based on what they've learned from the customer. So, in effect, every activity of the new organization will embed alignment, learning, and growth within it, from the Sprint to each area transformation to the overall culture shift for the whole organization.

Remember: Not Everyone Is Where You Are Yet

One thing that can happen is that when the leadership gets into the new mindset and makes it through the first couple of stages successfully, they feel like everyone else is there, too.

They can forget that some parts of the organization haven't even taken their first step yet. So, there's sometimes a disconnect when the leaders are so far ahead of parts of the organization that they forget to keep coaching the others through the process from the ground up.

This and other reasons can be why the transformation hits a plateau of sorts, which we call "Limited Agility."

THE LAST BIG PITFALL:
THE LIMITED AGILITY PLATEAU

Figure 10.3 Getting Stuck in Limited Agility

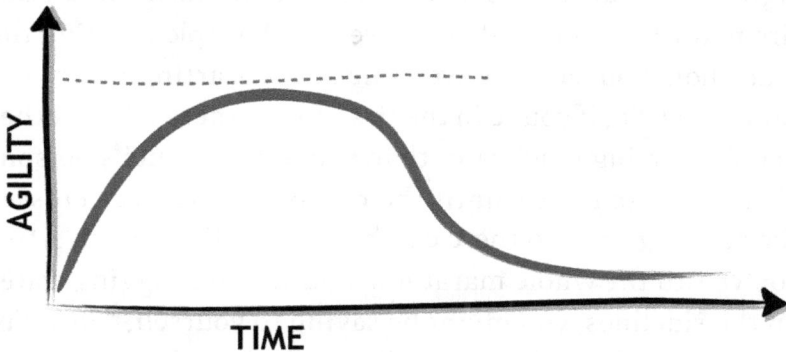

Limited agility occurs when organizations quickly adopt Agile practices and start "doing" Agile rather than making the time and effort to transform their policies to support the values and principles to the point of "being" agile. Thus, the practices are adopted, but the rest of the deeper issues remain. Unfortunately, the duration of the benefits of Agility are short-lived, and the organization typically returns to the traditional status-quo state over time.

As you can see from looking at Figure 10.3, you have a choice during this set of phases, too — one that will keep you on the path of sustained increase or set you up for Limited Agility, where you're still measuring your progress from the outside in and setting goals based on structure and process rather than culture and ongoing mindset shifts.

That's why, at this phase, when everything seems to be going well, you need to keep going.

Don't take your foot off the gas pedal or set your cruise control. You're not there yet. There is no "there" in terms of a destination. There's only a "there" in terms of a set of skills and knowledge, letting go of the past, and the new mindset to use them effectively.

I know I used a marathon runner as an example of what Agile isn't, but in this case, there's a similarity to an entire marathon in that if you have 5,000 people running the marathon, you can't fit everyone at the starting line at the same time. So, if you're in the first group, there will be other people starting much later than you. Each runner's personal time doesn't start until their Bluetooth tracker crosses the starting line. So there can be a weird disconnect. After you've run the whole marathon, and you're chugging water on the sidelines, you might be saying to yourself, "Hey, I'm finished, and I've been standing here for a half-hour. So, everyone's done, right?" But depending on how many runners there are, some people haven't even started yet! It's not over until everyone else crosses the finish line.

The transformation is like a marathon. Your area may have gone through the transformation, but other areas may not have even started yet. This is one of the times when anything can happen that could sidetrack success. Senior leaders leave, and new leaders bring new goals. Without someone continuing to spearhead the ongoing transformation, attention can wane, and the organization will stop before you get past that last plateau.

This is even more of a problem with very large organizations, whose transformations can take five to seven years overall. Even smaller organizations usually take 18–24 months to fully make the shift. A lot can happen from start to finish. For instance, one of our larger clients, which has about 40,000 people, has started down this path three times, and each time, they just stalled. They'd become partially Agile, but they'd get to a point where they would just not carry through with the rest, and then they'd kind of lose momentum and get to the same level of productivity as before — no gain. Part of it was their size. But the fourth time, they finally just decided to push through it, and they're all-in and really focused.

While the rest of the organization is still running the marathon, you need to be the person on the sideline with the megaphone, cheering for them to keep going. If you don't keep up their determination, the change plateau will stall your company's progress before the caterpillar can fully transform into the butterfly. Forced out of its cocoon too early, it won't do as well. It may have grown wings, but they're not strong enough yet to fly fast enough, far enough, or high enough. It won't survive for long against the elements, and all that time in the cocoon will be wasted. You won't see the gains you could have.

It's therefore important to make sure your optimizing goal remains at top of mind for everyone. To facilitate this, have your CLT hold periodic meetings with key influencers to keep everyone focused on the shift. Set up tactics for delivering information to the stakeholders and ensure those continue in some form throughout and beyond the transformation. Build a strong change leadership foundation that will withstand leadership and management turnover and continue the process with new people who are just as excited to make it happen. Think about it as a kind of succession plan for the transformation. If you have that in place, you'll have a much better chance of long-term optimization.

GETTING TO THE LEADERSHIP PRODUCT BACKLOG

Along the evolutionary line of Align, Learn, Grow, and so on, the items toward the later part are what most organizations never have time to get to. While you're spending most of your time putting out fires, micromanaging budgets, and minimizing the damage from waterfall snowballs-turned-avalanches, all those ideas for embedding innovation, coming up with better strategy, refining vision, developing a better-targeted set of products, and everything else you need to do long term sits on the sidelines.

Remember all those product backlog items your product owners had on the list? This is the equivalent in a leadership product backlog.

Now it's time to start bringing it to the table. Just as your product owners have prioritized their product backlog items based on customer need, you can start prioritizing your higher-level, more visionary items based on market forecasts, better value delivery, and other items.

Typical Leadership Backlog Items

Here are a few items that often come into play during the Accelerate and Sustain phases.

Portfolio Management

You're managing the portfolio of existing products in the current scenario. Now, from the long-term view, you can start looking at ways this can become more Agile. This goes back to the budgeting ideas I mentioned earlier. Do you want to budget in a traditional annual way, or does it make more sense to do it quarterly instead?

And what are you budgeting for? Projects or products? Or what about getting down to team-based budgeting? There's a whole book called *Beyond Budgeting*[24] about how traditional budgeting causes organizational dysfunction and how to go beyond that to a healthier continuous budgeting approach.

When you shift to Agile methods, you realize how much of a drain your budgeting activities can create. One problem creates another. What's intended to save money becomes a huge waste of money. Before shifting to an agility framework, one of our customers had an entire team of 12–15 people whose sole job, every day, was to look at all the work going on across the whole organization. They had a giant matrix of projects, people, and other details in a big Excel spreadsheet. And each of those little intersection boxes showed what was on track, off track, or ahead of schedule. If it was off track, they would have to figure out how to reallocate people with the right skills to a specific project. If it was ahead of schedule, they'd have to figure out how to reallocate back. If it was on track, they left it alone. So all day, every day, these people basically took status reports, which were complete guesses, and rejuggled the lives of people in project work groups. That was their job.

This is the Rube Goldberg machine in action. But it all stems from the same root cause: Project-related thinking and centralized budget management. When Agile comes along, that part of the machine becomes obsolete very quickly. That part of the machine, where the marble rolls down and hits the boot that kicks the toaster and roasts the marshmallow — just stops doing that. You don't need the boot and the marble. If you want to roast the marshmallow, just roast the marshmallow.

Strategic Innovation

Remember when I mentioned creating an intentional, structured process for innovation? This is the time to start including that in your operations. How can you create a pipeline of innovative elements, improvements, and functions? One way is to make these items part of the regular backlog and then have the teams start working them into their Sprints. Previously, your overstressed, overallocated functional teams never had time to think. But now, your Scrum teams have planning time embedded into every Sprint. Innovation is one way they can use that time.

You can also build other ways to capture innovative ideas and opportunities within the operational framework to create sources for the innovation pipeline, such as creating a team specifically designated to focusing on innovation. The ideas they come up with could become entirely new products, even reaching into or creating new markets.

Organizational Health

Now is the time to reassess your metrics for measuring this based on an Agile framework. Profitability is only one factor. Does your culture support the business values? Culture is crucial in achieving true agility. Are you able to be strategic, or do you spend too much time putting out fires? What kind of innovation practices are you embedding? According to Chris Zook, co-author of *The Founder's Mentality* and partner of Bain & Co., a management consultant firm, 94 percent of the barriers to achieving growth targets are internal.[25]

Many of these barriers, not surprisingly, are bureaucracy-related. But the real root problem, he says, is that the bigger a company gets, the farther away it goes from the founder's original vision. In other words, the values that created the company in the first place. This is, again, why culture is so important to long-term sustainability. It goes back to a fitness analogy. Is your focus for your organization the same as trying to lose a few pounds for the high school reunion, or are you really in the long game to improve your fitness and strength with the goal of improving your health and extending your lives? What do you need to measure from that perspective?

Systemic Improvement

What can you start looking at in terms of company-wide patterns and metrics that indicate things needing more attention? Where are things falling through the cracks organization-wide? How are your overarching processes supporting your new framework? Now is the time to delve into these things.

Multi-Team Collaboration

You've put some product-specific teams together and let them learn and grow in handling their specific product responsibilities. Now, what about getting them to work together toward the larger goals? For instance, what kinds of innovations could happen if you have cross-team collaboration? How else can your individual teams come together as a larger "team of teams"?

This approach mainly helps you get things done faster. To do that, it should be handled no differently from any other Agile team. Each team is cross-functional, and they're all working together to tackle different backlog items for the same product.

The goal is to have the lightest possible structure. No bureaucracy, no intermediaries. What you don't want to do is rely on people outside the team for collaboration. There's a particular concept out there for scaling Agile that tries to push Agile teams to collaborate within what is basically a waterfall structure. It's like putting a bureaucracy on top — and it just crushes the teams' effectiveness and their spirit.

When you have two teams, don't try to put a coordinator in the middle. Just let the teams talk to each other. They're self-organizing, cross-functional, responsible adults who are now charged with making sure they're coordinating together. Multiple product owners should talk to each other, and Scrum masters should talk to each other, but none are intermediaries for each other.

You Don't Have to Be a Unicorn

It's important to note that most companies don't get to the point where they're doing all these things well. In fact, it's really rare to see any of these achievements until the Optimize phase, which for the entire company is years out from the start of the transformation. So don't feel you have to achieve unicorn status and knock all these out of the park.

Even prioritizing one or two will bring value, especially if you identify what you need the most. That goes back to what you're trying to optimize for. If it's sustained growth, maybe you want to focus on organizational health to eliminate some of the problems preventing that. If it's customer value, maybe you want to focus on strategic innovation with the goal of delighting customers. Whatever you choose, as long as it aligns with your values and overarching vision/strategy, it will bring results.

CATALYST LEADERSHIP: LEARN TO LET GO

Business agility is ultimately a set of values embraced by the whole organization. As a leader, you can focus on tactical processes and worry about keeping people "utilized" doing their work, or you can focus on shaping values and serving as catalysts for engaging your people through those values. If you align your people to serve those values, you can let the process take care of itself in a more dynamic and responsive way.

Something interesting happens when you do this. You can let go... and the values take over. They are now in control. That doesn't create chaos; it creates more stability than you had before, and also more adaptability. You don't have to predict everything because you're already set up to respond quickly and naturally to new conditions.

As a leader, you are still needed for support and clarification on policies, values, vision, and overarching priorities, but your job gets a lot easier. You don't need to constantly loom over everyone to make sure they're doing their jobs the way you think they should. If they've embraced the values instilled in the culture, they'll know better than you do how to deliver the product value in support of those values.

The more you let go, the more your leadership team can become a C-level cross-functional team solving the high-level business problems that will support everyone else, rather than trying to manage the work. And you'll be a key member of that team. IT has huge potential to become a tool for excellence rather than a waterfall project nightmare. In this agility-focused model, you'll be a vital business partner and solutions expert in every major decision your leadership team makes.

Does this sound good to you? Because it sure does to me.

CHAPTER 11

SO, ABOUT THAT CLIFF...

A QUIET CELEBRATION

Around two years after our first meeting, Perry and I found ourselves getting together over a drink again, but this time, instead of coffee or tea, it was cocktails.

His teams had knocked it out of the park, saving more than $2M and coming in a year ahead of their original waterfall schedule (which, don't forget, was three years ahead in waterfall time). Needless to say, his business stakeholders were happier than ever. Perry had already held a big celebration with the whole organization the previous week, and this was a mellower but just as happy celebration of our own.

The two years had flown by. We were marveling at that as we sat in the corner of the little bar, reflecting on how things had gone and talking about the future.

"So, what's next?" I asked him, sipping my Ketel One martini.

He grinned. "I have a goal or two lined up."

He told me more about what was going on. Now that the new core internal system was in place, he could focus on some other more innovative products addressing customer self-service. His key stakeholders were excited. They'd patiently held on through the system migration with the understanding that some of their ideas and needs would come next. And after seeing how well the data migration had gone, they had full confidence that Perry and his team would be a huge help on the next set of initiatives.

The internal stakeholders saw Perry as a business partner who would help them achieve their goals, not a gatekeeper who was going to get in their way. He and his team had proven themselves ten times over. Not only that, some of the other leaders in the company were already thinking about how they could transform to more Agile methods, and they'd approached not only Perry, but also me, to see how they might start down that path.

It was definitely a win-win. He had gained the trust of his peers and leadership, his company was now in a better situation with the new system and agility methods in place, and I had some potential new clients interested in replicating Perry's success.

OK, make that a win-win-win.

While I don't always get to have a drink with every client who clears a huge hurdle like that, it's still great to watch. Every time, it's different in some ways, and it's the same in others. But one of the most satisfying things to see is how the people change and grow as they unlock their full potential, and how their lives invariably get easier.

I hope that's in the cards for you, too.

ONE KEY THING YOU NEED FOR THE JUMP

If you've made it here to the end of the book, I assume that means you're seriously considering a metaphorical cliff jump sometime in the near future, and you've found at least some of this material helpful in thinking about and planning for that.

I've tried to keep the information at a high enough level so that you can see the framework for planning without getting too caught up in or overwhelmed by the details of each element. Frankly, I could write a book for each segment in the AgileOS® framework. But you don't need that level of detail when you're starting out.

What you really need right now is the conviction that this is the way you want to go, and the understanding — at least on a basic level — of how the AgileOS® framework can make a difference not only in your department, but in your organization. You now should have that understanding from reading this book. Is it enough? Of course not. It's not going to give you everything you need along the way.

But it's what you need to move into the first step.

Remember, this process is iterative. You start on a foundation, and then you learn as you go, building and strengthening that foundation. Everything doesn't have to be perfect when you start, as long as you have the attitude that you'll learn and grow as you move forward. The information in this book has given you a great foundation, and your learning attitude will supply the rest as you go. Remember: You're unlearning the idea that you have to predict every little thing. Sometimes, you just have to set up all your initial gear to get you where you want to go — and then jump.

ONE OTHER THING I SUGGEST BEFORE YOU JUMP

I do want you to think about one more thing, though.

You don't *have* to do this alone. You can get help — with just about any part of your transformation, or the entire thing.

I advise considering that, not just because I happen to be in the business of helping in this way and am always happy to help new clients (which is true), but also because it's smart to involve someone from outside your organization who can look at it with a fresh eye and an objective viewpoint. Not having this element and trying to do it strictly from within is one of the main reasons companies stay mired in old habits and perspectives.

It's not that I don't believe you can do it. If I didn't, I wouldn't have bothered to give you a whole book full of ways to succeed. However, with help, you could potentially do it faster, with more confidence, and with better and more immediate results.

Many approach their transformation in a fragmented way, attempting to apply Agile training in one area or with limited focus on just the team. They may hire Agile trainers, not realizing that training is just the beginning. It can't address the full set of needs from a multifaceted, big-picture focus. Instead, it's more effective to hire a business agility consultant who can guide the entire transformation process.

Whoever you decide to work with (and I welcome you to check out Project Brilliant as you are doing your research), make sure you find the right fit for your needs and your particular organization. I suggest you work with a business agility consultant who meets the following criteria:

- **Familiarity with the entire picture of the transformation** (vs. just Agile training for your teams) so they can help you at least through the key components, especially the Align phase. I've shown you how crucial that is, and even that level of initial investment could save you a lot of headaches down the road.

- **Multilevel, high-quality Agile training for all levels in your organization** — teams, management, and executive level. Not all Agile training is created equal, and not all of it focuses on all levels to achieve total transformation.

- **Multidimensional, systems-thinking approaches** targeting key organizational aspects such as leaders, products, and teams to achieve successful transformation.

- **Broad knowledge and coaching expertise** in everything from Scrum roles to management considerations and **especially the expectations required at the executive level to ensure success**. Ineffective leadership is a key reason for failure; therefore, deep understanding of the C-level mindset and how it can lead effective business transformation is indispensable.

- **Deep familiarity with your industry,** especially if you deal with complex regulatory issues or other similar considerations.

All these elements will help ensure your overall success.

CONFESSION: I STILL LOVE THAT SAME PIZZA

OK, maybe not *every* night — maybe every few weeks — and definitely not in the same situation. This time, it's with my kids.

Still, I don't know what it is about ordering pizza, but my kids are the same as our old team. Every time we order, I swear we get the same thing. Everyone wants their usual — we may as well have a standing order.

And here's another confession: The pizza is even from the same pizza place — Donatos — where we used to order from so many years ago at that first crazy job I had. They say smell is a memory trigger, and I have to say that's true. Often, when I smell that pizza, I have flashbacks to those old days, sitting in my cubicle working till midnight.

However, the flashbacks don't bother me. In fact, I usually just smile a little because the pizza might be the same, but my situation has definitely improved, as in 3000x.

I would never go back to those days, or to any Rube Goldberg machine anywhere. You'd have to drag me kicking and screaming through the halls and chain me to the desk.

I actually have a life now. And it's pretty awesome. I get to do interesting work with incredible people. And, even when I do work longer hours, I don't mind because I see progress. I see momentum. I see huge things happening in incremental steps.

What about you?

You may not have the same pizza every night, but do you have the equivalent? Are you caught in your own situational version of the Rube Goldberg machine that's keeping you up at night, working late hours, managing micro details, and being asked to predict the unpredictable? Do you feel locked down and stuck, with no way out?

Maybe jumping off a proverbial cliff doesn't sound so bad after all. What have you got to lose except the predictability of the marble hitting the boot that kicks on the toaster?

Is it time to just start roasting the marshmallow and be done with it?

Only you can answer that. But I hope you seriously consider it. If you do, let me know. I'll be standing on the sidelines with my megaphone, cheering you on.

If You Feel This Book Was Helpful...

Authors are always looking for feedback. It's tough when your book goes out into the world, and you don't get to talk to readers to get their thoughts.

If you felt the material was useful, I'd appreciate it if you would take a couple of minutes to leave an honest review. Your comments might help bring the book to the attention of someone else who needs it, too.

Thanks in advance for paying it forward.

—Aaron

ENDNOTES

1   Stell Simonton, "Who Was Rube Goldberg, and What Are Rube Goldberg Machines?" *HowStuffWorks*, May 16, 2023, https://science.howstuffworks.com/innovation/famous-inventors/who-was-rube-goldberg-and-what-are-his-contraptions.htm.

2   "Domains of Business Agility," Business Agility Institute, accessed October 22, 2024, https://businessagility.institute/domains/overview.

3   "Principles Behind the Agile Manifesto," AgileMainfesto.org, accessed August 4, 2024, https://agilemanifesto.org/principles.html.

4   Jean Tabaka, "11 Ways Agile Adoptions Fail," *Agile Connection*, May 30, 2007, https://www.agileconnection.com/article/11-ways-agile-adoptions-fail.

5   "2023 Business Agility Report: Leading Through Uncertainty, 6th Edition, 2023," Business Agility Institute, https://businessagility.institute/learn/2023-business-agility-report/751.

6   Business Agility Institute, "2023 Business Agility Report," p. 18.

7   Business Agility Institute, "2023 Business Agility Report," p. 19.

8   Nasir Uddin and Fariha Hossain, "Evolution of Modern Management Through Taylorism: An Adjustment of Scientific Management Comprising Behavioral Science," *Procedia Computer Science* 62, (2015): 578–584, doi.org/10.1016/j.procs.2015.08.537.

9   Christopher Roser, "25 Years After W. Edwards Deming," *AllAboutLean.com*, December 20, 2018, https://www.allaboutlean.com/25-years-deming.

10 Roser, "25 Years."

11 Darrell Rigby, Sarah Elk, and Steve Berez, "The Agile C-Suite: A New Approach to Leadership for the Team at the Top," *Harvard Business Review*, May–June 2020.

12 Statistics presented at Gartner IT Symposium, October 2024.

13 "Priorities CIOs Must Address in 2025, According to Gartner's CIO Survey," Gartner, October 21, 2024, https://www.gartner.com/en/articles/priorities-cios-must-address-in-2025-according-to-gartner-s-cio-survey.

14 Gartner, "Priorities CIOs Must Address in 2025."

15 Business Agility Institute, "2023 Business Agility Report," p. 16.

16 Ken Schwaber and Jeff Sutherland, "The Product Backlog," in The 2020 Scrum Guide, Scrum Guides, https://scrumguides.org/scrum-guide.html#product-backlog.

17 Gartner IT Symposium, October 2024.

18 Stanley McChrystal et al., *Team of Teams: New Rules of Engagement for a Complex World* (Penguin Books, 2015).

19 "Van Niekerk Smashes World Record to Grab Olympic 400m Glory," Olympics.com, August 14, 2016, https://olympics.com/en/news/athletics-van-niekerk-smashes-world-record-to-grab-olympic-400m-glory.

20 "All You Need to Know about Relay Races: Rules, History, World Records," Olympics.com, https://olympics.com/en/news/athletics-relay-races-rules-history-world-records-olympics.

21 "ADKAR Model," Prosci, https://www.prosci.com/methodology/adkar.

22 "The 8 Steps for Leading Change," Kotter, https://www.kotterinc.com/methodology/8-steps/.

23 Linda Silsbee, "The Four Stages of Team Development," *Forbes*, June 29, 2023, https://www.forbes.com/councils/forbescoachescouncil/2023/06/29/the-four-stages-of-team-development/.

24 Jeremy Hope and Robin Fraser, *Beyond Budgeting: How Managers Can Break Free from the Annual Performance Trap* (Harvard Business School Publishing, April 11, 2003).

25 Chris Zook, "The Founder's Mentality: Leveraging Startup Thinking for Long-term Growth," Knowledge at Wharton Podcast, edited transcript July 21, 2016, 24 min., 20 sec., https://knowledge.wharton.upenn.edu/podcast/knowledge-at-wharton-podcast/160609b_kwradio_zook/.

ACKNOWLEDGEMENTS

First off, I'd like to thank my family for sticking with me through all my crazy entrepreneurial adventures these past years. To my wife, Kristen: You've been the stable foundation for our family through all the ups and downs of entrepreneurial life. Your willingness to take on that role has allowed me to do what I love in my work. Without your love and support, this would all have been chaos. And to my kids, Roman and Ruby, who've always been good sports when Dad goes away on yet another business trip, and always warm and loving when I return.

Also, a huge thanks to the many team members who've been part of Project Brilliant over the years. You've contributed your passion, skills, and knowledge with a level of dedication that has always reassured me that our clients are in good hands, even when I'm not there.

I wish I could name all the people who have taught me, helped me grow, and allowed me to be part of their own business adventures through the years — clients, friends, mentors, colleagues, in the Agile community and beyond — but that would probably be a whole other book in itself.

So I'll just say that you've taught me more than you know, and I'm honored to have you with me on my journey and to have been part of yours. I look forward to seeing what's further down our road together.

And finally, my thanks to Nicole Gebhardt and her team at Niche Pressworks for helping me make this book a reality. Your expertise and insight have been invaluable, and I couldn't have done it without you.

ABOUT AARON KOPEL

As the CEO of Project Brilliant, "Momentum Locksmith" Aaron Kopel helps guide leaders in their quest for business agility. With more than twenty-five years of professional experience, Aaron is one of only around twenty people in the world who hold the top four Scrum Alliance credentials: Certified Scrum Trainer® (CST®), Certified Enterprise Coach® (CEC®), Certified Agile Leadership Educator (CAL-Ed), and Path to CSP® Educator (CSP-Ed), and he was selected as a subject matter expert (SME) in the creation of the Scrum Alliance's CAS-Scaling (CAS-S) offering in 2023. He has a BA from Wartburg College (Business Administration – Management and CIS) and an MBA from the Kelley School of Business at Indiana University.

Aaron is a member of the Forbes Business Council (FBC) and founded the FBC Business Agility group; he is also a co-founder of several local/regional Agile communities, including AgileIndy, Agile Fort Wayne, Agile Dayton, and Agile Louisville. A two-time tech startup entrepreneur and National Science Foundation (NSF) grant winner, Aaron has a background that spans from small local to large global companies in industries such as technology, finance, medical device manufacturing, pharmaceutical manufacturing, publishing, general manufacturing, healthcare, and early-stage software and product development.

Aaron is well-known for his engaging and interactive workshops that simplify complicated business and leadership topics through creative visuals, memorable stories, and witty humor. His passion for history and travel has inspired him to visit more than fifty countries to date, and he's also known for his fanaticism for the band Pearl Jam (forty-five concerts and counting). Aaron currently lives in Carmel, Indiana, with his amazing wife, Kristen, and their two teenagers, Roman and Ruby.

CONTACT

Website: ProjectBrilliant.com
Email: Agile@ProjectBrilliant.com
LinkedIn: LinkedIn.com/In/AaronKopel

Locked down
by status quo?
Feeling stuck, and no matter what you do, you can't break free?

CIO Momentum Intensive
45 days to unlock the status quo and build momentum!

Create Keys	Unlock Barriers	Get Moving
Solidify your personal leadership pillars and catalyst mindset.	Identify and unlock the barriers holding you hostage.	Establish your optimizing goal and build momentum.

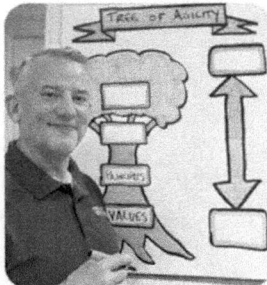

The Momentum Locksmith®
CIOs locked down in regulated industries struggling to escape the status quo look to Aaron Kopel, the Momentum Locksmith®, to help them become a better partner to their business, unlock the potential of their organization, and build momentum toward a brighter future.

LEARN MORE

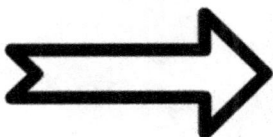

www.ingramcontent.com/pod-product-compliance
Lightning Source LLC
Chambersburg PA
CBHW071559210326
41597CB00019B/3310